THE GENTLEMAN'S
ART OF DRESSING
WITH ECONOMY.

ĐEDICATED

TO MY OLD AND *TRUSTY* FRIEND,

𝔄. 𝔗𝔞𝔶𝔩𝔬𝔯,

TO WHOM TO HIS *CREDIT* BE IT SAID)

I SHALL CONTINUE TO OWE

AN ETERNAL DEBT—OF GRATITUDE.

THE AUTHOR.

Megatherium Club, Pall Mall,
May 1876.

THE GENTLEMAN'S

ART OF DRESSING

WITH ECONOMY.

BY

A LOUNGER AT THE CLUBS.

First published in 1876 by Frederick Warne & Co, London

This edition published in 2012 by
The British Library
96 Euston Road
London NW1 2DB

British Library Cataloguing in Publication Data
A catalogue record for this publication is available from
The British Library

ISBN 978 0 7123 5886 6

© The British Library 2012

Printed in Hong Kong by Great Wall Printing Co. Ltd

PREFACE.

———◆———

THE preface to a book, like the name of a baby or the sign of a public house, though often thought of, is seldom decided on until the supreme moment arrives when the vexed question must be definitely settled; and now that I am brought face to face with the difficulty, I find, like CANNING'S Needy Knife-grinder, that I really have no story to tell, further than what is embodied in the book itself. I may remark, however, that there has been a marked progress in the style of gentlemen's dress within the last few years. Whatever defect artists may find in it—for, confessedly, there is an absence in male attire of those waving and flowing lines so desirable in the delineation of the Beautiful (fancy the Apollo Belvidere in a waterproof Ulster, or Adonis with knickerbockers and patent roller-skates on!)—yet for ease and comfort, the costume now in vogue (yᵉ hat of yᵉ period excepted) cannot be much improved on.

Those who remember the dress of forty years ago, as I do, are able to appreciate the change. The saying that midshipmen dress with a needle and undress with a pocket-knife might be applied to the costume of that day. The tightly-fitting trousers, strapped closely down and hauled up "taut," to the total preclusion of all sedentary occupation, were a walking pillory, while the buckram-stiffened cravats were literally stocks. Wellington boots were donned by pulleys, and not doffed without machinery. Waistcoats were worn double, the under one usually of a lemon tint. The coat, which was entered by a hand-to-hand fight, was purgatory to wear, and deliverance thence was little short of a miracle. It consisted chiefly of collar and brass buttons, and, like the Line tunic of this day, was neither useful, ornamental, nor reasonable in price. Obviously, on these grounds, it held its own, for years, against all comers, according to true Conservative principles.

The cheap tailor of the day, aided by the sewing machine, has been a great reformer and leveller of class, breaking down the social distinction which formerly separated men in dress. At present it is impossible to distinguish a gentleman by his raiment only; and whatever gradations of rank may exist in this country, I consider it an advantage that *primâ facie* all should appear equal, and entitled to class themselves as gentlemen, so far as outward and visible signs may go. Even to be mistaken for a gentleman may often give noble aspirations, and induce a man to try and "behave as such."

The cynic who said Eve sinned that she might dress has not enlightened us as to Adam's motive for so doing. Surely it was not the same. Granted that Eve got tired of perpetual *Buff à la mode,* and that her Godiva polonaise ceased to be a novelty, we cannot imagine that Adam, with his great mind, went a-hankering for man's millinery—prone after Paletôts, Ponchos, and registered Pardessus. We can understand the fair sex being much concerned with dress, nor should men grumble at the attention they give thereto; for, after all, it is a tribute to the lords of the creation, for whom it is done to please—ladies, of course, being never actuated by a desire to eclipse each other! but for a man to devote his heart and soul to the art of bedizening is to write himself down an ass — a most conceited ass.

Between the coxcomb and the sloven, however, there is a gulf as wide as between the Good Templar and the Dypsomaniac; and without being either, the practical man may be glad of a few hints both on dressing and economy.

If it be true that he who causes four blades of grass to vegetate where only one grew before benefits his race, surely he who shows those "with verdure clad" how to drape their manly frames to greater advantage and in the guise of gentlemen, cannot be said to write in vain.

CONTENTS.

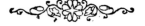

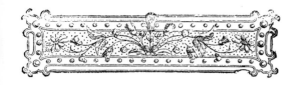

THE ART OF DRESSING.

CHAPTER I.

INTRODUCTORY.—ON DRESS.

Pre-Adamite man—Adam's dress—The Picts—The Cad—
The Snob—Swells—Gentlemen's style—Club men—Bishops
—Priests—Parsons—University men—Officers—The Valet.

WHETHER pre-Adamite man was ever clothed, and in his right mind, we wot not. Geological research throws no light on the question. Philosophy is silent on the matter, and history on this subject, of course, does not exist. However, one thing is certain

1

that since the day our progenitor Adam adopted
the fig-leaf as full-dress regulation for his garden
party in Mesopotamia, the necessity for costume
ever after became a fixed fact ; and whether it be
in Asimbanaboo, where spectacles and a cocked
hat are exacted by an over-prudish society for
fêtes champêtres, down to the shady side of Piccadilly, where existing police regulations, and the
changing varieties of our clime, demand some-
what more diffuse covering, the adoption of
garments of some sort is now universal.　How
the Picts of yore managed to pull through without contracting pleuro-pneumonia may well as-
tonish the speculative mind.　I am no judge of
painting, so cannot estimate the comfort of their
costume, but imagine the worst-cut garment of
this day would have competed on good terms,
with something in hand to spare, with the most
brilliant coat of woad erst worn by them. Whatever hues the males may have adopted—among
the ladies of that day what variety of colours
and diversity of tints must have existed, numerous, no doubt, as the prismatic effects of the
rainbow ; yet it may be questioned, picturesque
as they must have looked, whether the style
which obtains with the fair sex of the period is

not superior for hygeian purposes to that of days gone by. Fortunately, the ladies of the nineteeth century use no paint! Now that Madame Rachel has been improved off our stage, the art of being "beautiful for ever" has fallen into desuetude, and rouge and Rock of Sahara are neither known nor called for.

It might prove entertaining and instructive to trace the different steps and stages in the development of dress, from the pristine fig-leaf down to the registered Ulster of our time, and applying to the subject the Darwinian theory of selection, demonstrate how the fashion for leaves faded, while knickerbockers survived in the struggle for existence.

This little manual, however, aims only at being a practical guide to dress—not an æsthetic work on costume; so we must forego the pleasure of pursuing this subject further, and content ourselves by observing that, although the primary objects of dress appear to have been utility and warmth, these quickly gave way to finery and ornamentation. So we find in tropical climes, where clothing is not a vital necessity, the aborigines have, according to their unpublished *Follet,* set fashions for wearing their anklets, bracelets, rings, and beads, and the laws of their fashions are, no doubt, as inexorable with them as they are with us.

To come *per saltum* from the Garden of Eden to Middlesex—from Paradise to Pall Mall—we are struck by one important and melancholy fact: Adam, the initiator of dress, had no tailor's bill to pay, but has entailed on us the curse of either running an account for ours, else—there is no alternative—of paying cash on delivery for our clothes! Dress thus proven *de rigeur* all the world over,—

> "From Greenland's icy mountain,
>   To India's coral strand"—

the question naturally arises, How shall we dress, and wherewithal shall we be clothed? The answer I give is, Let us dress like gentlemen; and the object of this *brochure* is not only to teach how this may be done, but how it may be effected with economy.

Now, "cheap and nasty" being terms seldom possible to dissociate, you will bear in mind, dear reader, I by no means propose to turn you out "a howling swell" for next to nothing, but simply to show you how, in dress, you best, for money, may get your money's worth. So our subject is to be considered under two heads:

1. *How to dress as a Gentleman.*
2. *How to do so with Economy.*

As to the first. Simply wearing good clothes will not constitute dressing as a gentleman; for the cad, the snob, and pretentious swell may all be superfinely clad, but the garb of a gentleman is not known to them.

In my youth I remember a book of dietetics, entitled, "What to Eat, Drink, and Avoid." Concisely it told you to take the best of everything, and to shun carefully all inferior food. The advice no doubt was good, and I shall apply the idea by showing some styles of costume which must most studiously be eschewed.

Let me try a pen-and-ink sketch of the three types above mentioned.

The cad comes first. He is, in Mr. Bright's favourite language, the *residuum* of third-class counter-jumpers; he blossoms freely on Sundays and other holidays, and makes the streets hideous by his presence. His outward and visible signs are as under: shiny black frock coat and black pants—the former buttoned awry, the latter short, with legs of uneven length; hat related to the fretful porcupine; embroidered shirt unregenerate; green satin scarf, stabbed with mock pin of coloured glass set in brass; gloves of startling hue, with an unexplored territory toward the finger-tips.

Such is the cad—caddy.

The snob, on the other hand, wears clothes elaborately cut and of novel design. There is much "drawing," as artists say, about his dress. He takes for model the stock music hall so-called comic vocalist, and affects thunder-and-lightning trousers, pegtoppy, or in the other extreme of horsiness; slap-bang coat, broadly lapelled, buttoning at the umbilical region. His hat may be new, but savours of Stratford-atte-Bow—not of the *ateliers* of Bond Street.

If on good terms with his laundress, he puts forth his linen shirt-front and cuffs *en evidence*, else covers up the one with a vast expanse of satin scarf, donning "reversibles" to do duty for the other.

Such is the snob. Copy him not.

The swells may be divided into two classes: the swell proper (or English *gandin*), who tries to dress well and succeeds; and the pretentious swell, who tries to dress well and don't. His is a style carefully to be eschewed. It is not easy to describe its peculiarities; but would you see it, to take not for an example, but as a fearful warning, visit the *buffets* of some fashionable City restaurants, and observe the loudly-dressed young men flirting with sensation barmaids who serve therein, and you may study the type to (im)perfection.

The swell proper is faultless in his attire, so far as cut, fit, make-up, and material go; but unfortunately leaves the impression that he was made for his clothes, and not his clothes for him. Nor does he wear his dress with ease : he appears afraid of wrinkling his coat when he moves, and of knee-ing his pants when he sits, and too frequently *poses*, that the crowd may see he has taken toil and trouble to produce an effect.

Dressing thus is dressing as an artist to illustrate costume, but decidedly not dressing as a gentleman. In fact, no one should aim at looking like a dressed block in a ready-made tailor's window, nor appear as if melted into the clothes upon him.

Dr. Johnson, Shakespeare, or Nicodemus—I forget which—alluding to a man as being the best-dressed of his acquaintance, was asked why.

Answer was because no one could remember nor describe any article of dress he wore. Whoever made this remark was an undoubted authority on the art of dress, and one with whom I would gladly confer, were it possible, on the subject matter under discussion. Search through the number of your own acquaintance for a well-dressed man, and having found your *beau idéal* (or real) of the same—on examination, it will turn out that the most perfect type is remarkable for an absence of "loudness," both in colour and in style; and as a person with passable features is said to be able to go through a crowd without frightening any one, so a well-dressed man may be seen daily without eliciting criticism one way or the other on his costume. Herein lies the secret of success; and if you understand how to do it, it will be unnecessary for you to read these pages further. *Ars est artem celare,* and this knack of dressing is essentially an art: to a certain extent it is innate; and if you have it not naturally, it is not easily to be acquired. But, *àpropos* of Johnson, as we have introduced his name, would he not have said, "Sir, let us take a walk down Fleet Street"?

Well, Temple Bar being in a rotten state and

my life not insured, suppose we change the venue
—or avenue, if you prefer it—and let us have a
stroll in Clubland, where we shall see some of
the best-dressed men, if not in Europe, at least
in London.

I do not assert well-dressed men are indigen-
ous to the West-end, to the exclusion of other
parts of town, nor claim for Pall Mall and Piccadilly a monopoly in fashion. Men in the unmistakeable garb of gentlemen may be seen in all
parts of London, all over England, and elsewhere. What I contend is that in the world of
Clubland you find concentrated a set of men of
some social position, who mix freely in society, in
salons, among the *élite* of rank and fashion. If
their dress will pass muster in the places they
frequent, it ought surely be good enough for us
to copy and take a lesson from.

Along Pall Mall we walk, and observe those
going in and out of its palatial halls. First we
pass the OLD MAN CLUB, and perhaps you may
not be struck by any great display of dress by
those who frequent it, for remember, this asylum
is only eligible to those of F.O. rank, who, having
passed their *première jeunesse*, may be supposed
to have renounced the pomps and vanities of

attire.   Yet note the neatness and precision of
nearly all—from their well-brushed hats down
to their glossy boots, which, though often roomy
for the gouty, are polished so that on emergency
you might shave yourself therein.   And here we
may learn our first lesson in the art of dressing,
namely, military cleanliness.   The majority of
members of this club have been swells in their
day, and many of them may have led the fashions in their youth; and now in the evening of
life, even in the sere and yellow leaf, they retain
the habit of precision and neatness—bearing out
the old saying : " What's young learnt is never
old forgotten."

THE MINERVA CLUB opposite will not afford
us much insight into the object of our research.
Its *clientèle* are too deeply engrossed with Greek
roots, fossil remains, and Professor Huxley's
theories, to spend much time over the cut of a
paletôt, or the flowing lines of sixteen-shilling
Sydenham trousers.   But if you wanted an historical essay on the *tunica* or *toga* of the ancient
Romans, with notes critical and exegetical thereon, pointing out the length and material of the
former, and the varieties and significations of the
latter—many of its learned members would be

found competent authorities on these matters. With classic acumen they could descant on the *gens togata* or *togati*, accurately distinguishing between the cut and finish of the *toga prætexta* and the *toga virilis.* The trimmings of the purple worn by the conquering hero on his triumphal entry would be within their ken ; while you and I, I fear, know nothing whatever about these matters, except that from this word *toga* we derive the slang terms "togs" and "toggery."

THE VOYAGERS adjacent is also of that ilk— a cross between the Old Man and the Minerva —no scandal meant anent the goddess !

The next club to it may, perhaps, claim the credit of having inaugurated, as the slang term goes, "REFORM IN TAILORS' BILLS ;" and, although microscopic research might detect a percentage of well-dressed men within its walls, better remain yet to see.

Now come we to the stately TORY CLUB and its younger brother opposite—THE JUNIOR TORY. We dismiss them in a word by saying their members are more noted for their strong political proclivities than for any organized attempt to impart *ton* to the world of fashion.

THE OXBRIDGE AND CAMFORD, next on the

list, teems with the parson element ; shovel hats
and aprons abound, and make one wonder what
the *raison d'être* of the latter garb may be. " How
much prettier," said a lady to me the other day,
on meeting a real live bishop, " it would look if
the dear man had it *ruched*, or wore it full kilt-
plaited in the front." Talking about the clerical
tribe, I have often wondered why the garb of
holiness should be black ; for as this hue is
commonly associated by us with his Satanic
Majesty, it might not be unreasonable to expect
the celestial uniform to be of quite another tint.
Church dignitaries would be more consistent and
more complimentary to their calling were they
to turn out like angels, in colours "ever bright
and fair," instead of draping their reverend frames
in materials " black as the ——— ! " But this, however, is more a question for Convocation, and
really is not any affair of mine.

At that little symposium, sacred to the officers
of Her Majesty's Brigade of Guards, are many
well-dressed men ; and at the well-known RAG
may be seen, *me judice*, the best-dressed men all
round in town. Going farther afield in Clubland
we may fare worse ; but continue our walk up
aristocratic St. James's Street, and get a notion

of 'VARSITY style at the CLUB so-called. Then cross the street, and peradventure you may see, in the bay-window of NOODLE'S, some rare old fossil of a Noodleite, carefully preserved, tawney and crusted—dressed in the style fashionable fifty years ago. Few remain now; yet you may come in for the sight. Yes! by Jove! there goes old Lord X—— in tightly-buttoned bright blue coat and brass buttons; coat-collar about a fathom deep; cravat knotted in a manner that Beau Brummel might have approved; he is be wigged and be-dyed, puffed, powered, padded, and would sadly miss stays if he left them off. Although a thing of beauty and a joy for ever, I do not counsel you to imitate his mode of dress.

A saunter round St. James's Square brings us back to the RAG, and allow me to reiterate, that here the best-dressed men do congregate.

Officers in the service may easily dress well— they have many facilities for so doing. They go to good tailors to begin with—although I do not consider, as a rule, that the best military tailors make the best mufti. Their profession necessi- tates frequent change of their clothes throughout the day, and uniform bears the brunt of the wear —the most damaging to good clothes—sitting at meals, with an occasional shampoo of gravy, and lounging cross-legged after dinner. Last, and certainly not least, officers all possess that most inestimable benefit in the way of valet — the soldier-servant, who cleans, dusts, damps, brushes, and folds their clothes as soon as taken off, carefully putting them away until further wanted.

What cannot a regimental servant do with regulation pipeclay? In his hands it is omnipotent over cloth. He can charm stains and grease-spots thereout, even as an Indian juggler charms snakes; and what sleight-of-hand he exercises over your garments generally! The coat, grimed and mud-bespattered, is beaten with switch or cane, and, when folded away, comes out as from a press. Trousers, baggy at knees as the historical parachute of dear old Mrs. Gamp, are manipulated into their former shape. Compared to the private valet, always expensive and frequently mutinous, he is a pearl of great price. His cost is a dole; and, thanks to that excellent institution the regimental guard-room, he can always be kept within control.

Having shown you the dress of gentlemen by example rather than by precept (for there is no sealed pattern of it), we pass on to our second head.

CHAPTER II.

HOW TO DRESS WITH ECONOMY.

Economy—Credit—Ready money—West-end tailors—Economical tailors—Cut—Fit—Make-up—Keeping clothes in shape—Repairs—Price list.

HIS subject of economy is a wide one, and might be treated to the nth power of x in diffuseness. So, to avoid prolixity, and yet do justice, as I intend, to the question, I shall divide it into four heads (like that un-disestablished infliction, the Sunday sermon of the day), and after discussing each, shall make some practical remarks, which I trust may go home to the hearts of, and prove a lasting blessing to, my readers.

They are as under:

1. You must pay ready money for your clothes.
2. These must be well cut and well made up.
3. They must be kept in shape.
4. They must be kept in thorough repair.

The word economy, I may remark, is often misunderstood, and frequently misapplied. The primary signification of it is (from the Greek words *oikos* and *nomos*) the law of the household, whereby the prices of all articles of consumption should be familiar in one's mouths as household words all the year round. In the received and vulgar acceptation of the term, it means the art of getting things cheap. Now, getting things cheaply merely because articles are low in price is no part of economy. Ladies are greatly given, in their rounds of shopping, to buy goods they could thoroughly do without, because they purchase them, as they fancy, "cheap."

In buying anything and everything, two questions must invariably be asked :—

Can I do without it ?

If not, can I get it for its fair value ?

If you can do without an article, and buy it notwithstanding, you do not buy it cheap let its price be what it may ; and if you purchase what you want, and give more than the market value for it, you do not succeed in obeying the law of economy. For a blind person to buy an expensive painting for his own use would be a perversion of economy, the same as it would be for a man with two wooden legs to subscribe to a rink, and buy a gross of Plimpton's roller-skates, in the hope some day he might be able to use them. Nor is it economy to buy for a low price an article you cannot do without. You may only give a trifle for it, to find it turn out worthless. No ; the practical meaning of economy is the art of buying what you know to be a necessity of good quality, for which, while the world is a world, you must be prepared to pay a fair market price.

To plunge at once in *medias res*. To dress with economy you must adopt the ready money system. If you run a tailor's bill the thing cannot be done. Your credit tailor not only sticks it on in price, but is often careless about fit and make-up, especially if you are so deep on his books that he guesses you are not in a position to pay him off and go elsewhere. Again, the *haute volée* of tailors cares little for your custom unless your yearly account is considerable; and although the most aristocratic snip is not above

making you a single coat, the same attention is
not bestowed on it as if you gave an extensive
order. Even from the work-rooms of Burlington,
Albany & Co. I have seen many a solitary coat
turned out that would scarcely have passed
muster in a ready-made Mosaic clothes-shop.

And here I may recite what is not generally
known anent the credit system.   The West-end
long-credit tailor seldom or never loses by bad
debts, for he has on his books many customers
who neither pay ready money nor ask on order
the price of the clothes they get.   At the end of
the year, in addition to charging 5 per cent. on all
outstanding accounts, they reckon up their debts,
and divide the sum total of those who are not
able to pay among those able and willing to do
so.   With them, therefore, the game is a strictly
paying one.   " Heads," they are sure to win;
" Tails," there is no possibility of their losing.
Again, when they wish to realize their capital,
and call in what money they have out, they in-
vent the legal fiction that one of their partners
is seceding from the firm, and as a settlement
must be effected, they are reluctantly compelled
to request you to close your outstanding account;
but, they add, when this pleasant transaction is

carried out on your part, they will be ready to continue the business as heretofore; and with thanks for your patronage, they solicit a continuance of your esteemed custom, and beg the further favour of your kind recommendation.

In "Punch," many years ago, appeared a sketch, by John Leech, of a swell giving an extensive order to his tailor: he says to him (I quote from memory), "Brown, ha! I want some coats." "Yes, sir. How many may you please to want?" "I'll have six—no, I'll have seven. And, Brown, I want some twowsers." "Yes, sir. How many pairs will you allow me to send you, sir?" "Twenty-four pairs — and, look here, Brown, show me patterns that won't be worn by any of the snobs." *

It by no means follows that you will dress well by merely giving an unlimited order to a

---

* "Mentioning "Punch" reminds me to remark that if you have been absent from the world of fashion for a time, and wish to know the style of dress in vogue, you cannot do better than consult the pages of our facetious old friend. Therein you will see the exact costume of the day, in all detail, from hat down to the very boots. There is no more truthful indicator of fashion published; and when Mr. Punch's artists depict *a gentleman* of the period, you will not be wrong in following suit.

first-class tailor. Money alone will not insure this consummation, nor is a gentleman's turn-out necessarily in direct ratio to his outlay. I know men who spend pounds on dress where others spend shillings, without appearing to much greater advantage. You may dress expensively without dressing well, as you may dine expensively and not dine well. To dress well and to dine well, both require TASTE to an infinite degree, and he who exhibits most judgment in the selection and harmony of his dishes and garments will be the best-dined and best-dressed man.

The question may, perhaps, now be asked by the reader, " If I am not to patronize Messrs. Burlington, Albany & Co., or an *artiste* of similar calibre, to what tailor shall I go ? " Well, it is not my province to recommend any particular tailor or tailors ; you pay your money and take your choice; but without mentioning names, there are hundreds of excellent economical tailors in London who turn out clothes equal in style and cut to the above eminent firm at prices from 35 to 40 per cent. lower, so cannot afford to give credit for longer than three months. To this class I should go. They may be found in quiet streets off the most fashionable resorts, and invariably have been cutters or foremen to the *dii majores* of the sartorial art. As a rule, they make no show, nor exhibit anything in their windows. A brass plate on door, or blind in front, tells their trade. Inside you find a private work-room, hung with brown paper patterns, and perhaps but little stock of cloth. This is what I like. A tailor of this stamp has always, in addition to his own stock, the latest pattern-book from the leading London wholesale houses, from which you may select; and if you prefer seeing other materials in the piece, as many do, then he will direct you to some of the well-stocked cloth-shops, not a hundred miles from the Albany, where you may wander through groves of newest designs until your fancy "feels the fulness of satiety." On giving him the number of the piece, he will get it and make it. Thus he can have no object in foisting on you last season's patterns, nor obsolete cloth he may have in stock. Another great advantage is, a tailor of this class is his own cutter, and will attend to any little peculiarity of cut you may desire. In large establishments the man who takes your measure may not perhaps cut nor see the garment ordered.

Avoid " stripping pegs," as the phrase is, or buying ready-made clothes. A skilful attendant at any such depôt has a knack of pulling down, smoothing, and humouring whatever garment he may set his great mind on selling you ; so that before the cheval glass, you look as if you had been born therein, and you and it both grew on together. Ah, dear delusion ! You pay for it, and pass out. After a little wear you find the smooth gracefully-fitting robe becoming restive. It kicks up its heels, and plunges at the collar to displace your hat ; it puckers, wrinkles, and makes you its bitter enemy so long as you continue to wear it. " *Poeta nascitur non fit*," remarked " Punch " years ago, in allusion to a poetical and advertising outfitter. *Verbum sap.* Go to a skilled tailor ; order your clothes ; fit them on ; and you will thank your stars for taking my advice.

I am not writing exclusively for Londoners ; but as every one nowadays comes up to London on the slightest provocation—making it an excuse to have one's hair cut—and as all wish to appear to best advantage when in town, I advise those who visit modern Babylon to have their clothes made there. I say this by no means to the disparagement of provincial tailors—many of whom buy the best cloth and employ the best workmen that can be got. Nevertheless, I am free to confess and contend, as learned counsel say, that clothes made out of London are re-dolent of country tailoring, and have not the *timbre* which belongs to style and fashion. There is a *je-ne-sais-quoi* about a West-end London cut unmistakeable; and I advise my readers, if they must needs patronize the local rural snip, to employ him on shooting coat, fishing garb, or costume intended for country wear exclusively.

"I know," says Mr. Trab to Pip in "Great Expectations," "that London gentlemen cannot be expected to patronize local work; but if you would give me a turn now and then in the quality of a townsman, I should greatly esteem it."

Avoid everything *outré* in fashion—whether it be in material or in cut. Seek not to copy swells who lead the fashions, and sometimes affect eccentric garments and fancy stuffs — (witness the Noah's Ark coat, long exploded; and more recently the dress coat of blue cloth and brass buttons). Such vagaries may do for men of means, who can afford to wear their clothes a short time and then discard them; but you stick to a coat cut on unflinching principles, which will not be out of date next month or next year.

Make-up is a most important item in tailoring. It chiefly affects braid, buttons, button-holes, and linings. I have seen many a coat, of first quality and unexceptionable cut, spoiled by want of care in making-up. Braid is often put on unevenly, too tight, or too slack ; and in either case the coat must pucker. Attention must be paid to skirt-linings, which should exactly coincide with the cloth : if wider, even a trifle, the skirts curl outwards ; if tighter, they must curl in. Button-holes are frequently scamped, and the intervals between parallel rows of buttons on coat-fronts do not always correspond.

N.B.—If you can afford the time, do not allow your coats to be sent home without calling at your tailor's for a final try-on.

Ready money, cut, and make-up having been discussed, we next come to keeping clothes : 1, in shape ; 2, in thorough repair.

In the due observance of these lies the great secret of dress ; for economy is not effected so much in the original purchase of clothes, as in the subsequent wearing of them. What a well-developed talent some men have for taking the

shine out of new things in a few days! By ex-
cessive lounging, leaning, and lolloping about,
they pull off proof impressions of furniture on
their backs, elbows, knees, and other frictional
parts of the anatomy!

Now, if you do not keep a **valet** (and if you
wish to dress with economy, you had better not)
you must either be your own valet, or get some
one to do the work. NO CLOTHES, HOWEVER
NEW, WILL LOOK WELL UNLESS KEPT IN SHAPE.
This is done by folding them carefully up the moment you take them off. Next morning or the day
after will not do. The reason is, while the cloth
has the warmth of the body in it, it is more plastic
and impressionable than when cold. I have
seen many persons throw their clothes down in
a heap, to put them on next morning all in
wrinkles. Of course, if you chuck your things
in a stack to stagnate into creases, and put them
on "with a pitchfork," there is no hope of your
ever looking well dressed. I grant it takes a
little time and some trouble to turn out spic and
span ; but once the habit is acquired of folding
your clothes away, it becomes a second nature,
and well repays the outlay.

I said above, clothes must be folded *carefully.*

There is a right and a wrong way in this as in everything. Each garment must be pulled into shape before folding. The coat-sleeves should be gently but firmly stretched to full length, and then doubled up with the crease at elbows. The skirts are then turned over, and, without disturbing the collar, the whole is doubled down the back, and left at full length when put by in wardrobe.

This mode differs from folding for packing. In this case the collar is turned up, arms doubled, skirts brought up to collar—cloth to cloth; the process then goes on as above. Trousers should be pulled down each seam, and particularly stretched from fork or crutch to boot; then fold them flat, *knee to knee*—not as tailors do, with crease down the centre; then turn over into three, taking care this crease is below the knee.

To keep trousers in shape, you should occasionally damp them with a sponge well wrung out. When folded, envelop them in brown paper, and put away under a heavy trunk or other weight. How do soldiers, with their limited stock of trousers, manage to turn out so well? Simply by following these directions: they damp their overalls, roll them up, and place them often under their bed or pillow.

When clothes are wet, they must not be folded —only pulled into shape and put to dry. A coat is best placed over the back of a chair, as if dressing a lay figure ; trousers over a towel horse. This will be found better than hanging them from pegs, for they are apt to dry askew and out of shape. Often after drying it will be found they require a tonic to restore them ; and the tincture of iron (hot) must be administered by a tailor, unless you can have the 'remedy applied at home. Here it is where ancillary help comes in handy. Mary Jane, if willing and a skilful *repasseuse*, should be suborned with a largesse of ribbons or similar fal-fals, and instructions given her to iron on the wrong side only—previously having damped the refractory garments with a moist sponge.

Of all enemies to clothes the most deadly known is dust. If you have been caught in a whirlwind of it, you will fold away your clothes in vain. They must first be dusted. Mark well : if you wear cloth ground in with dust, and are caught in the rain, your suit is done for. You must have a limber switch or cane borne on the effective strength of your toilet establishment, and make free use of it at the end of a dusty day.

If you don't like the job yourself—and few do—
(for it is neither a lively nor intellectual occupation, and a frightful incentive to thirst, at utter
variance with Sir Wilfrid Lawson's and all Good
Templars' doctrines)—you must get it done by
the handmaid — the domestic Abigail before
alluded to—or by any one else you please, so
long as it is done.   However, I repeat—dusted
the clothes must be, or they will be done for.

We now come to REPAIRS; and it is impossible
to exaggerate the importance of keeping your
wardrobe in thorough working order.   No matter
how well built and rigged a ship may be, A 1
registered at Lloyd's, copper-bottomed, high
above the diphthong—even up to all Mr. Plim-
soll's requirements ; after a voyage she must
be docked and refitted ; so a well-dressed man,
after his clothes have been some time in wear,
must repair to his tailor for repairs.   It comes
expensive to employ the original artists and de-
signers of your costume for small jobs : indeed,
they seldom care to do them, and yet the work
must be done.   " The time to mend the plough
is when the plough is broken," and in the matter
of repairs it will be found that the proverbial
stitch in time saves, not nine, but nine-and-ninety.

For this purpose look out for working tailor, bootmaker, and hatter in your own immediate neighbourhood, close to home, who are not above doing these small jobs and executing trifling orders off the reel. They may be found readily in London, in bye streets off the main thorough-fares. For ready money payments they will, at a trifling charge, keep your kit going. The tailor will rework button-holes, mend linings, finedraw holes made by rent or burn, renew buttons, &c. The bootmaker's services should be requisitioned whenever there is the slightest wear perceptible at either toes or heels of boots. The hatter is often wanted to smooth the nap when ruffled by storms of rain, adverse winds, and hostile umbrellas. I know, as well as you, you can get a hat ironed for nothing at the hatter's where you deal. But it often happens after a stormy day, if not passing his way, you neglect the hat, or attack it furiously yourself with a hard brush—to no purpose. After a few days the gossamer thus treated is condemned as shabby, or sent by parcels delivery to the maker, who washes, re-binds, and re-lines it at the cost of five shillings; while sixpence in money and five minutes in time, expended on a working hatter, would have obviated all necessity for this. And so on with other small matters. This is a fair illustration of our subject, and will show what prompt action in repairs will effect. Your linen, too, must be kept duly posted up to the time of day, and if you have not wife or—well, say maiden aunt, or other female friend, addicted to the art for which Penelope was famed, then you must take sweet counsel with your laundress, and bribe her when necessary, to have the edges of your shirt-fronts and wrists machined, which are easily done at a trifling cost. I have often seen men, otherwise well dressed, mar the whole effect by exhibiting frayed cuffs, which simply wanted new running with a hem.

In this little book I have not attempted to lay down any fixed rule as to how much yearly one should spend on clothes. So much depends on the wearer, in the first place; secondly, on the stock of things one has in hand to start with; and thirdly, on the judicious selection of new material. I append, however, four tables of prices of clothes, of all descriptions required of tailors under ordinary circumstances; and the reader may elect to make what choice he likes. No. 1 shows top price charged by West-end tailors to West-end swells on the credit system. No. 2 shows same quality on the ready money system, or, much the same thing, three months' credit. No. 3 gives second quality, and second-rate work, for cash; and No. 4 is slop-shop price, ready made and ticketed in window.

No. 1.

(FIRST QUALITY ON CREDIT: SAY FROM THE EMINENT FIRM OF MESSRS. BURLINGTON, ALBANY & CO.)

						£	s.	d.
Frock coat	...	...	...	...	...	7	7	0
Vest ...	...	...	...	...	...	1	10	0
Trousers ...	...	...	...	...	...	2	5	0
Dress coat	...	...	...	...	...	7	7	0
Do. vest	...	...	...	...	...	2	2	0
Trousers	...	...	...	...	...	2	10	0
Morning coat	...	...	...	...	...	5	10	0
Vest ...	...	...	...	...	...	1	10	0
Winter overcoat	...	...	...	...	...	8	8	0
Suit of dittos	...	...	...	...	...	6	10	0

£44 19 0

No. 2.

(FIRST QUALITY, READY MONEY SYSTEM, FROM CLASS OF TAILOR RECOMMENDED.)

						£	s.	d.
Frock coat	...	...	...	...	...	5	0	0
Vest ...	...	...	...	...	...	1	0	0
Trousers	...	...	...	...	...	1	8	0
Dress coat	...	...	...	...	...	4	4	0
Do. vest	...	...	...	...	...	1	1	0
Trousers	...	...	...	...	...	1	15	0
Morning coat	...	...	...	...	...	3	10	0
Vest ...	...	...	...	...	...	0	15	0
Winter overcoat	...	...	...	...	...	4	10	0
Suit of dittos	...	...	...	...	...	4	4	0

£27 7 0

No. 3.

(SECOND QUALITY, AND SECOND-RATE WORK, FOR CASH.)

						£	s.	d.
Frock coat	...	...	...	...	...	3	3	0
Vest ...	...	...	...	...	...	0	12	6
Trousers ...	...	...	...	...	...	0	18	0
Dress coat	...	...	...	...	...	2	15	0
Do. vest	...	...	...	...	...	0	12	6
Trousers	...	...	...	...	...	1	0	0
Morning coat	...	...	...	...	...	2	5	0
Vest ...	...	...	...	...	...	0	12	6
Winter overcoat	...	...	...	...	3	0	0
Suit of dittos ...	...	...	...	...	3	0	0
						£17	18	6

No. 4.

(SLOP-SHOP TARIFF—READY-MADE, OR "THIS STYLE TO ORDER"—NOT RECOMMENDED.)

						£	s.	d.
Frock coat	...	...	...	...	...	2	5	0
Vest ...	...	...	...	...	...	0	10	6
Trousers ...	...	...	...	...	...	0	13	0
Dress coat	...	...	...	...	...	2	0	0
Do. vest	...	...	...	...	...	0	10	6
Trousers ...	...	...	...	...	...	0	15	0
Morning coat	...	...	...	...	...	1	15	0
Vest ...	...	...	...	...	...	0	10	6
Winter overcoat	...	...	...	...	2	0	0
Suit of dittos ...	...	...	...	...	2	5	0
						£13	4	6

As it would serve no useful purpose to discuss every item in the above four tables, I propose to devote a chapter to each article of dress, appending, in "Conclusion," some practical remarks on our subject generally.

CHAPTER III.

COATS.

The frock coat—Newmarket coat—Overcoats—The Chesterfield
—Summer Overcoat—The Ulster—Norfolk jacket—Dittos
—Inverness cape—Full-dress evening coat—The surtout.

F all coats the FROCK COAT is, for morning wear, the most dressy and fashionable. It is pre-eminently the garb of a
gentleman, and should be worn by gentlemen
only. The snob and the cad in a frock coat look
snobbier and caddier in this garment than in any
other you can name. The frock coat of the day
is invariably made of fancy cloths, diagonals, or
twills, to the exclusion of Meltons and plain-
faced stuffs. To my idea, whatever be the texture of the cloth, the frock coat in colour should
either be black or blue. Nowadays it is made

in light fancy materials—lavender and grey twills or French crape. After all, it is merely a matter of taste; but to my eye these materials do scant justice to the frock, which is *par excellence* the King of Coats.

To those who study economy, however, it has many disadvantages. It must be of first quality. Second quality will not do. It is indispensable that it be lined with silk, the skirts especially, or they cling to the legs, and give it a dragging, wrinkled appearance. It must be of exquisite cut, make-up, and finish, and requires careful putting on, and a good graceful figure to carry it. Persons of stout, dumpy build, round-shouldered, or of slouching gait, should not wear it. If this coat be of inferior quality, it gives the wearer a poverty-stricken look; and if A 1 in all particulars, it necessitates equal perfection in all other garments. Hat, trousers, boots, shirt, tie, must be prepared to bear strict scrutiny—even gloves and umbrella must correspond in excellence. As you must go to a first-rate tailor for this coat, I do not think any hints necessary about its make, except, avoid the skirts overlapping behind, or, what is worse, opening from the waist downwards, like the letter V inverted.

In my day I have seen the fashion of this coat change perhaps a dozen times—sometimes short-waisted, sometimes long; now short-skirted to one extreme, anon long-skirted to the other. Be this as it may, you must have no fixed idea of your own on this matter, but follow the prevailing fashion in the frock coat as well as in your style of hat.

———

THE CUTAWAY COAT.—This coat, formerly called the Newmarket, is the most profitable for every-day town wear, and may be worn either double or single-breasted : the former best for spring and autumn, the latter for summer. For long wear Melton cloth is to be preferred to the ribbed and diagonal twills now in fashion. These readily take up dust, are difficult to keep clean, and soon wear white at seams and frictional parts. Melton cloth is not so dressy, but, unless worn out, never looks shabby. When new, have this coat made up with plain edges, or edged with round braid, called piping. After some months' wear, when the coat requires doing up, a heavy broad silk braid may be laid on. This will change the whole character of the coat,

and it will look, even to the wearer, like a new one.
Do not have an outside breast-pocket. Stuffing
a handkerchief in makes it bulbous, and puts it
out of shape. No occasion for silk linings,—
Italian cloth will do. The coat should be cut
full to the lowest waistcoat-button before being
rounded off. As a rule, the front is generally too
much cut away, which gives it a scamped look.
This remark applies to single as well as double-
breasted.

As to colours, none are so serviceable as black
and blue, and you cannot be far wrong in selecting either, as they always are in fashion. Fancy
colours come and fancy colours go, but black and
blue go on for ever. For town wear especially,
I recommend these two to be adhered to for
the ordinary morning walking coat. However
fashionable mixtures may be in the country or
in provincial towns, they are not the "clean grit"
for London wear; and if you wish to do in
London as the Londoners do, avoid all motley
patterns for your walking coats.

The regulation length of skirt of morning coat
may be determined by letting the arm fall to the
side, with fingers extended. Then the ordinary
skirt is level with the tip of the middle finger

A short skirt comes to the nail of little finger; a long one *à discretion.* Remember, in skirt proportion the same rule holds good which relates to the nasal organ; for is it not written, "An inch in a man's nose makes a great difference"?

———

OVERCOATS.—The most serviceable greatcoat is what is called the double-breasted CHESTERFIELD. This should not be cut too sacky or baggy behind; and to look smart, the length must not extend below the knee. The front of this coat should be bold, not skimpy or pinched in cloth, buttoning well across, lapels large, and the pocket-flaps (not too deep) made to go in or out of pockets. This coat may be made in almost any stuff, but the most serviceable cloths are dark blue, claret brown, and invisible green. Avoid fluffy, woolly, nappy materials : they look well when new, but wear out quicker than a smooth-faced finished cloth. This coat, when new, can be worn with collar of its own stuff ; when button-holes require re-working, have put on a velvet collar, and the appearance of the coat will be materially changed. Always have two inside breast-pockets to this

and every coat, and distribute your cargo throughout all the pockets.

———

THE SUMMER OVERCOAT.—This is "a great
boon," as Artemus Ward remarked about the
Tower. There is scarcely a day all the year
round when an overcoat cannot be worn with
comfort in London during some portion of the
twenty-four hours. No matter how hot the days,
the evenings chill down, and a light surtout will
be found not out of place. There is no end of
variety in these coats. Many of them are to be
avoided as worthless. Noticeably among the
number are the dust-coats for races, which burst
out like ephemeræ about the Epsom week, and
disappear as suddenly as those neuropterous
insects. Indeed, it is a curious question what
becomes of the gossamer diaphonous garments
alluded to. Many start for the Derby in them,
but who ever saw their return to town? Do they
melt away in transit and become absorbed into
the system, or do their owners throw them away
out of thorough shame at their vulgarity? Waste
not your shillings on such trash! Have a sum-

mer coat built by a skilful tailor, and do not
strip a peg for one under any consideration.

The summer overcoat may be cut single or
double-breasted at your pleasure. If the former
style be adopted, let the button-holes be cut
through for the buttons to show—not in paletôt
fashion, which is only worn by clericals—and let
it lap well over to the right side in lieu of buttoning straight down the middle, for in this case the
lapels must look scamped, as if the cloth had run
out.

A very pleasant coat for summer wear is one
cut on the double-breasted Chesterfield lines, but
made to wear singly, without one underneath.
During the scorching Sirius it can even be worn
without a waistcoat, and will be found deliciously
cool and self-ventilating for this purpose. Inside
pockets should be cut below the facings for watch
and petty cash, and if gold Albert chain be worn,
a loop of silk braid to hold the same should
not be forgotten. This coat is solely adapted
for walking, and obviously will not answer for
prandial purposes. It might prove awkward if,
clad in it, you dropped in to dinner with familiar
friends, where lovely woman graced the board,
and were asked to remove your overcoat as a

preliminary. Even at a bachelors' party it could scarcely be considered *en régle*. But then it only professes to be adapted for one end, and aims not at being all things to all men. In fact, it is impossible to design a garment which will meet the requirements of all circumstances : to lounge in during morning—look fit for the Park in the afternoon—dressy at a five-o'clock tea in Belgravia—suitable on emergency for a fashionable dinner party—and not out of place in the stalls of Covent Garden in the height of the operatic season. If you can point out to me the tailor who has invented such a coat, I shall patronize him at all hazards.

THE ULSTER.—This useful overcoat was the invention of a tailor and draper in the Emerald Isle, and on its merits quickly became popular through the United Kingdom. Originally the coat was made of the best material only; but now the tailoring fraternity have "boned" the "notion," and their shops are flooded with so-called Ulsters, which may be bought at almost any price. I have seen them ticketed as low as twenty-one shillings. The stuffs used in these ultra cheap coats might be useful for straining peas — indeed, a closely knitted antimacassar would afford as much protection to the body — but then they are made, like Peter Pindar's razors—only to sell! Now, a good Ulster is a wonderful boon for travellers, for they can not only dispense with railway-rugs, but carry, as Wemmick might say, "much portable property" about the person. But the cheap coats above described are a miserable mockery, and would be dear even at a gift.

A custom has obtained of late of wearing these Ulsters for peripatetic purposes, and many may be seen in fashionable parts of London. Of course, in wet or snow there can be no objection to them; but on the other hand, they are as well adapted for a promenade as a mackintosh would be for a full-dress evening party. Even in foul weather, however, I doubt their utility for walking purposes. In rain or snow the long skirts quickly get saturated, and take long to dry. In fair cold weather, when a brisk quick movement is desirable, they impede the action of the spindles and make locomotion a nuisance. On the subject of Ulsters, I may note an ingenious improvement on the original design. The coat is made in two parts. The upper story is the old original pea-jacket, the under one is a capacious skirt which buttons to it underneath.

The rage at present is for THE IMPROVED ULSTER, to which my attention was first called in the "Field" newspaper of the 1st January, this year. Instead of being shapeless as a sack, it falls in easy graceful lines, rather fitting to the figure. The contraction round the waist is effected solely by the band behind, and vest, trousers, and undercoat pockets can all be reached without going through the process of unbuttoning—someway on the principle whereby an officer's scabbard is passed underneath his military overcoat, with the advantage that the opening is fully protected from the wet. Then, to show how crude inventions are improved to absolute perfection, there is contrived, out of sight on the arm, a pocket, in which a lady can insert her hand while walking arm-in-arm with you, thus keeping her fingers from being frozen. Here is an advance in science! Here is a grateful combination of the *utile et dulce*—especially the *dulce!* What cavalier, under such circumstances, would object to hear whispered to him in dulcet tones, "Oh, what a muff!"

THE NORFOLK JACKET, for sporting purposes or general country wear, is deservedly a great favourite. It is generally made with one pleat down each side of front, and from one to three behind, as the wearer may elect. Pleats in the dual number are most effective for ordinarily good figures. Three give an appearance of breadth, while one imparts that of height. Capacious pockets can be furnished in the folds, and the belt which circles the waist can be pleated into cloth cases to hold cartridges. This arrangement, however, gives a clumsy effect to the Norfolk, and should not be ordered unless for this specific purpose.

KNICKERBOCKERS of the same material are very generally worn with this style of jacket; but, in addition to them, I recommend you to order trousers, and the choice between the two will often be appreciated.

Hats made of the same stuff as the breeks and jacket are good form, and quite *en rapport* with the above style of dress.

DITTOS, as they are called, consist of coat,

trousers, and vest of the same stuff. They are fashionable for country wear, but must not be worn in town. The round hat belongs to this costume, with which the tall chimneypot is inadmissible. The recent fashion is to have the pants of different material. This plan is better, for the coat and vest will outlive the trousers. The coat should be full in front, not too long, the back same shape as the undress blue patrol military jacket. This coat cannot have too many pockets: two inside, two outside, breast—flaps, two in skirts and one ticket-pocket. It is never bound with braid.

In choosing materials for dittos, of course you must be guided by the season for which you may require them. It is said light-coloured clothes are cooler in summer, because they reflect a portion of the sun's rays; and they are warmer in winter, because they do not radiate the heat of the body so rapidly as dark clothing. Dark-coloured clothes are warmest in summer, because the darker the cloth the more perfectly it absorbs the direct heat of the sun. They are, however cooler in winter than light-coloured clothing proving the rapidity with which they absorb the heat from the body.

I advise you to select quiet mixtures in preference to any of the howling patterns of the
day. Some men turn out striped like zebras, or
ruled off into diamond lozenges or mathematical
squares ; and such suits once seen will be ob-
served, and will only lead any one who may take
the trouble to remark, to wonder how long their
owners will continue to wear them.

THE INVERNESS CAPE.—This is an antiquated
garb, and has been completely superseded by the
Ulster, which popular Hibernian has put many
other noses out of joint : to wit, the Poncho, the
Pardessus, and the Upper Benjamin. One sample
of the latter garb, I believe, may still be seen in
a window in one of our leading thoroughfares,
where it has been on view, to my own personal
knowledge, now wellnigh twenty years.

THE FULL-DRESS EVENING COAT. — This,
like the frock coat, must be of first quality, made
by first-rate tailors. The skirts should be full,

à la d'Orsay. Two inside pockets will be found convenient.

Although there is little of this coat, it is not easily made to fit perfectly. Unless it "catches" on the shoulders it will hang shapeless, with as much symmetry as an ordinary pump-handle. It must be lined throughout with silk; and the secret of its success lies in having the length of tail regulated according, not to your height alone, but to your figure. With the dress coat I prefer trousers, not of ordinary black, but of dead twilled rifle cloth, which shows off both coat and patent leather boots to great advantage.

———

Both Chesterfield overcoat and double-breasted Melton morning coat will bear turning, which can be done by a working tailor at the cost of eighteen shillings. The coats will do for second best, but should be differently trimmed with braid, buttons, &c., on tergiversation.

A single-breasted coat will not turn, for the obvious reason that the button-holes would appear on the reverse side.

Any man built on great fundamental prin-

ciples should avoid flap pockets on the hips.
The pockets must be behind in coat-tails.

———

THE SURTOUT.—This is a large edition of the
ordinary frock coat, and is a very elegant and
dressy garment. Like its younger brother, it
should be of best material and make. The cloth
most adapted for it is called "velvet beaver." I
prefer a shade between dark blue and purple.
This coat is not so serviceable as the Chesterfield, nor so comfortable. The pockets are behind, and not so handy for reference to one's
handkerchief in cold weather ; nor can you get
your hands in them for warmth—a practice I do
not recommend, for it drags the coat out of shape
—yet, like many other things, unfortunately,
though "naughty, it is nice."

The surtout is seldom done justice to, and
liberties are often taken with it—in this way :
This coat should be cut to wear either alone or
strictly as an overcoat. Now, some people try
to make it, like Oliver Goldsmith's celebrated
chest of drawers, "a double debt to pay," and for
this purpose it is eminently unsuited. If cut for

single wear and dragged over a morning coat, its shape is strained ; and if made for overcoat and worn alone, it is safe to look baggy and sloppy in the back.

The regulation length of skirt for the surtout is to the end of the knee-cap.

"*Chacun à son goût,*" says the proverb; and this being a free country, every one may follow his own fancy in dress as in other things. I, for one, do not dislike, but simply hate, overcoats trimmed with fur collar, facings, and cuffs. If the cold be extreme, a real Russian pelisse is a comfort and a luxury; but for a Whitney cloth to be faced with a selvage of fur is false heraldry, akin to the impious snobbery of having electro-plated articles with silver mountings, wherein the main body of the manufacture is of base metal, and the meagre trimmings real—one halfpennyworth of bread to the vastly disproportionate amount of sack. Again, this style opens the door to that never-to-be-sufficiently-reprobated fashion, in vogue with cads and others, of wearing imitation fur, seal, and Astracan. Real fur, &c., is bad enough, but what shall we say about mock? Even the jackdaw in the fable, held up to universal ridicule for his borrowed plumage, went in like a bird for real expensive feathers, scorning dyed stuff as beneath his notice.

To wear imitation anything is contrary to the rules of high art, too repugnant to the feelings of a well regulated mind. Nothing mock will ever go down with gentlemen—except mock-turtle, and even this at best is only a malicious libel on the true delicious esculent.

CHAPTER IV.

WAISTCOATS.

Material — Single and double-breasted — White vests — The Chamois vest.

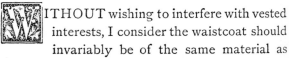

WITHOUT wishing to interfere with vested interests, I consider the waistcoat should invariably be of the same material as the coat. Some wear vest and pants alike, but the effect is not so good. Again, the vest is certain to last longer than the trousers, and then you have on hand a garment that may ill assort with any other of your wardrobe.

Fancy stuffs for waistcoats I do not admire, nor see I any advantage in having vest of texture different to your coat.

Vests are best made without collar, or with a dummy one—that is, the outline of it, designated either by braid or stitching. You thus avoid all lumpiness at the back of the neck, which disarranges the sit of coat-collar in that neighbourhood. Take my advice, and have four pockets in every waistcoat. The upper side-pockets come in very handy : one for a few loose sovereigns— the other for railway ticket or latch key.—*Apropos* of this, pardon a parenthesis. Some persons mix up gold and silver promiscuously in their purses; others carry silver only in pockets—gold and bank-notes in their purse. The best plan is to carry notes only in your purse. When you change a fiver, transfer the sovereigns to side upper vest-pocket above mentioned ; and when you change gold into silver, carry the latter in right-hand lower waistcoat-pocket—watch in left ditto. The advantages claimed for this system of banking are that your money is never mixed. You cannot drop a bank-note in taking out gold, nor in the dusk give a sovereign for a shilling to a confiding cabby. Again, in public places, you need never show money, nor let strangers know how much you have about you. Many a robbery has been induced by the incautious exhibition of a purse's contents. A light-fingered gentleman seeing one change a modest half-sovereign, might

not let his "angry passion rise" for so small a
pelf; yet the same *prestidigitateur* would likely
exert all his art for the balance one had about
one if he only saw it.

DOUBLE-BREASTED WAISTCOATS are not
favourites of mine; but if you like them, wear them
by all means, and we shall not be worse friends.

WHITE VESTS are not only dressy, but luxu-
rious for summer weather. Take care to have
them of good quality and well cut. *Avoid the
cheap ready-made sort, which show their machine
origin in every stitch.* They never fit—are impossible to iron—and wholly unsuited for gentlemen.
At present white grounds with fancy stripes are
more worn than plain white, and not being made
of common material, look more fashionable. Both
kinds are expensive, requiring washing and the
services of a clever laundress to make them up.
If too much starched, they crack and sit badly; if
too little, they freely take the dirt. White waistcoats made of paper are advertised, but hitherto
I have been mercifully spared the infliction of
seeing them. No doubt they are sold and worn;
but I infer the cad class only wrap their unclean
persons in such pulpy atrocities!

On the subject of vests I cannot help record-

ing my approval of an under-vest made solely of
CHAMOIS LEATHER. Of course, it is neither for
show nor ornament, but is designed to take the
place of the clumsy and, to my mind, slightly
snobbish seal-skin, being equally warm, and cost-
ing a tenth of its price. This vest is cut double-
breasted, to button across the chest right up to the
neck, with long sleeves to wrist, and in length may
be six inches below the waist. It is intended to
be worn over the white shirt ; and, as it will only
be used in extremely cold weather, it will be
covered from view by the scarf; but by throwing
the lapels back, as much shirt can be shown as
you please. This garment will be found to have
all the warmth of a great coat—(" Mr. Guppy is
of opinion 'decidedly more so,'")—while for light-
ness and bulkiness no comparison can be insti-
tuted. It will last for years, and being worn over
a shirt, does not require washing, but may be
renovated in the course of time by a leather-
dresser, without subjecting it to the cold water
cure—a process which coddles the chamois, and
extracts the goodness or virtue from it. Any
tailor, draper, or professed shirt-cutter is competent to make this vest. The price of it is about
a guinea, and I recommend it with great confi-

dence to weak-chested folk suffering from pul-
monary or pleuritic complaints, lung disease,
phthisis, bronchial affections, asthma, and to all
that numerous class of persons who are known in
the graphic language of the turf as " confirmed
roarers."

CHAPTER V.

TROUSERS.

Price—Cut—Fit.

 RAPID stride of late has been made in the art of cutting trousers. Twenty years ago I remember a few tailors in London (not many) were supposed to have a speciality for making them. These select few, I may remark, did not neglect to charge for their special knowledge. Fifty shillings per pair was their general charge, although they condescended occasionally to make for their more favoured customers some cheap trousers for two guineas. I don't know what occult influence the introduction of pegtops had on the science of pant-cutting; it may be only a coincidence; but I date from the time those ridiculous overalls came in and went out, a new era—in fact, quite a revolution—in the style of trouser fitting. Most tailors now can cut these garments, but, owing to low prices charged, few are well made up. The cheap trousers, say from thirteen shillings to eighteen shillings a pair, are not only not shrunk, but positively stretched, to make the stuff go as far as possible. The seams are run with the sewing machine, and, "from information received," I believe only one shilling a pair is allowed for making them. This accounts for gaping flys, pockets of network, and buttons barely tacked on, and then generally in wrong places. If these cheap trousers don't fit, tailors won't alter them. The contract price will not admit of this. They sell them like penny rolls in a baker's shop—take or leave them.

I consider it a gigantic waste of money to pay two guineas, and upwards, for "bags," as they are facetiously called; nor can I conscientiously advise the adoption of the ultra cheap pantaloons. Then comes the question where to draw the line between the best and the worst. In Table 2 you will see at a glance what pantaloons of first quality should cost, and these being worth the money, will be found the cheapest in the long run, and may be depended on for durability and comfort. Should you ever happen, when absent from London, to want new trousers on an emergency, and are ready to take trouble, I will initiate you into the secret of obtaining good trousers, well made, at a strictly moderate price.

You must first be the happy possessor of a pair of trousers entirely to your satisfaction in cut — fitting without a fault — perfection itself. If they are sufficiently worn "not to owe you anything," as the saying is, have them ripped, and a pattern made of them in brown paper. Get a duplicate of them, and keep in your own possession, as tailors have a knack of mislaying or losing them (if wanted back) either by design or accident. Now find a working tailor (the one who does your odd jobs) and ask him to cut your unmentionables strictly according to pattern. Mind! he is not to measure you, nor put a tape around your manly form. Some self-conceited snips will stand on their dignity, and say they served their time with Brown, Jones, & Co., or other eminent firm of trouser-makers, and from the pattern shown will predict utter dis comfit and misfit if followed. If your lot be to meet with such, there is no use giving them the commission. They will do all they know to spoil the pants. You must search on until you find one ready to carry. out your orders with integrity. The next step is to select your materials in some wholesale cloth-shop, and purchase enough stuff for three, in textures unlike in colour and in make. This must be sent home to yourself in the piece, to be operated on in the following way:—The stuff bought must now be soaked in a bucket of water, in which is put a handful of salt, which will effectually prevent the colours running. You must insist on the immersion, and not take it for granted as done: ocular demonstration will be necessary. The cloth is then hung to dry thoroughly, and when dessicated, is sent to your trusty snip to be cut according to pattern, basted, fitted on, any little errors corrected, then finished and hot-pressed with iron on wrong side only. By this process you insure your materials against shrinking: for some trousers, long to-day, after a shower of rain will shrivel into knickerbockers on the morrow. You get them cut on the lines after your own heart, and as to expense, the following is a fair estimate for three pairs:

Cloth, seven yards, at 6s.— 42s., enough for three pairs. Cost of making, say in country quarters, 8s. per pair—24s. Thus you have for 66s. three pairs of trousers, which is only a trifle more than Messrs. Burlington, Albany, & Co. would charge for one.

There is a hint for one in search of economy in dress; but as this plan entails much trouble, I do not expect to see it extensively adopted. On the other hand, under similar circumstances, absence from London, &c., it is equally applicable (bar the cold water cure) to morning, walking, and overcoat. More caution, however, and greater confidence in your tailor will be necessary than for trousers; for you may chance to get your cloth spoiled in cutting; then, as the garments are altogether at your own risk, you must stand the racket in having them thrown upon your hands. I have come across intelligent tailors (of the type under discussion) capable of successfully imitating West-end coats at very moderate prices. However, I should never think of trying their "'prentice hand" on frock or dress coat; and I confess they are better left alone altogether, except as cockboat or *dernier ressort*.

For trousers to fit well, it is of first importance

that they be well up in the fork, and reach right down to the ground. Short-legged trousers defeat all attempt at trying to appear well dressed. If muddy, turn them up (fortunately it is the fashion to do so nowadays), and have the back edge round the heel inside bound with a slip of morocco leather, half an inch deep, which should be flush with the bottom of the legs. This prevents their cutting with the ground; for in this case they cannot be let down should they shrink in wear.

Trousers should be cut to fall straight from the knee (plumb-line), with a slight spring over boot. The width over boot is invariably one inch and a half wider than knee measurement. Most tailors fail to hit off the *juste milieu* at the termination of their trousers, and make them either too gaitery, like the bottom of a caraffe, else slope them away horsey, or in ostler fashion. Let this rule be a guide for you. Suppose you wear elastic-side boots, for example. See that the line from back of heel is horizontal until clear of the elastics (*inside* as well as out) before the cloth is sloped away. Tailors generally commence hollowing out as soon as the cloth is clear of the boot-heel. This is a radical error. The

line I have indicated should be prolonged one
and a half inches on both sides before you begin
to turn the royal arch.

One word about material, another about patterns. Avoid soft nappy cloths: the pile quickly
wears off, and the trousers look threadbare.
Choose firm, strong tweeds. Some are like pin-
wire, and wear practically for ever.

In patterns shun checks, plaids, and chess-
board devices. Never order any material so
prononcé that you would know it again. Stripes
in long parallel lines are to be avoided : when
the knees get ever so slightly baggy, the break
in continuity of the lines draws attention, and
makes your pantaloons, though only out of shape,
look shabby. Pepper-and-salt, light and dark
brown, and all grey mixtures devoid of any decided pattern, will be found most serviceable,
and are always fashionable.

Do not wear the same trousers two consecu-
tive days. If you have a good stock, keep a
roster, and let the first for duty take its turn.
By this means they will always look fresh, and
not hackneyed.

CHAPTER VI.

BOOTS.

Good—Bad—Indifferent—Boot-trees—Polish—Waterproofing.

X pede Herculem, — You may gauge a great swell by his boots. If this translation is too free, anyway it has the merit of truth.

Cæteris paribus, the extremities of dress are most important; and if these are shabby, you must look *in extremis.* A good hat and good boots are the Alpha and Omega of a well-dressed man. As to boots, you are more liable to be taken in in these than in any other article of dress. Of course if you can afford to deal with North, Humber, Land, & Co., you run no risk of getting inferior boots.

Non cui vis contingit adire Corinthum,—All
purses can't pay Piccadilly prices for shoe-leather.
So, if economy be an object, you must deal elsewhere. Now, if you purchase boots promiscuously—that is, anywhere—you are likely to be
let in for more bad pairs than good. The boot
market is flooded with trash of all sorts, made
up for the eye, and not for the feet. The worst
feature in this arrangement is, that unless you
are in the trade, or know something about it, it
is impossible to estimate the value of the article
you buy. As I know a little on this subject, I
may mention some boots to be avoided.

There is one sort, machine-made, without welts,
and soles riveted on—not one stitch in them.
You may be let in by good-looking Northamp-
ton work, with soles to all outward appearance
capable of resisting a deluge, but which, in reality,
consist of a thin outside of leather, which covers
in bits and dabs of padding—as a Whitechapel
cigar, beautiful to the eye, is but an envelope of
tobacco crammed with tea-leaves and decayed
garden produce. Then there are French boots
and shoes, imported in immense quantity, lovely
to look on, but bootless for wear. I am assured
the soles of these are composed of leather shreds

acted on by some solvent, and rolled into sheets by heavy pressure. In wet or moderately damp weather, they melt like ice before the fire, and are incapable of being mended.

The best plan is to go to a good bootmaker— one long established—who has his leather laid in some years to season, and get your boots to measure. Once he has fitted you to satisfaction, purchase the lasts, and have your boots made thereon ever after. In price you must not expect to get good boots too low. Thirty shillings per pair is a fair price all round. For wear, I question the economy of buying any cheaper. If you want fit and style, you cannot get them for less.

To have your *chaussure* on a good footing, you should possess a goodly stock of boots kept in thorough repair, and renew them as they are done for. Six pairs of boots to start with, worn in rotation day by day, will last longer than ten pairs bought singly and worn out one after the other.

Always get hand-stitched boots in preference to clumps or pegs. They are more comfortable and wear longer, being in general made of better stuff.

Break in new boots by wearing them frequently in the house before trusting yourself out in them a whole day at a stretch. How many a pleasant "outing" has been spoiled by too confidingly putting on new boots in the morning! Oh! the aching at midday—oh! the agony in the evening. No joy can compensate for the misery of tight boots. Even Rosherville, proverbial for "a happy day," will fail to soothe the afflicted soul tormented with pedal callosities!

You will find the due cultivation of the boot-tree will bear much fruit. Trees are indispensable for boots when wet—to restore them to their shape. Their use keeps wrinkles out and prevents boots cracking in the uppers. Avoid wearing the same pair of boots two days running, or walking. If damp, it punishes them severely to use them until the soles get dry and harden; besides, they will not polish while wet, and the servant (orders to the contrary notwithstanding) is safe to put them close before the fire or on the oven to facilitate their shining, which mode of treatment both cockles the leather and takes the goodness out of it.

If you wear elastic-side boots, do not have them made with mock buttons or imitation lacings. Avoid fancy filagree machine stitching and boots of grained goat-skin or crinkled leather. They are never worn by gentlemen, but obtain great favour with cads and snobs. Should I be honoured by lovely woman glancing over these pages, I would say the same style of boot worn by her sex is ill adapted to any above the social rank of general servant and Mile End mantuamaker.

Light laced boots or shoes, to look dressy, should be made up without brass eyelets, and the best silk laces used.

Would you be dry-shod in snowy weather? Purchase a dip candle, and before the fire rub it into the welts and uppers as far as the galoshe, also the soles themselves, and "rough" them afterwards with two or three small brads hammered half-way in. This is preferable to the ordinary waterproofing sold in shilling tins, which requires much time to apply, and generally cracks the leather.

In putting by summer or winter boots for six months to come, anoint them freely with goose grease if you can get it; if not, use dubbin—but gander fat is better.

One word more on boots, and then my subject

will be completely polished off. When patent leather begins to lose its lacquered brilliancy, its case is past liquid renovator or French varnish. Have them blacked and polished. You will find this plan answers best; and for all boots use the liquid blacking in jars, which is more preservative for leather than the paste. The latter, I am told, often contains an undue quantity of oil of vitriol.

MATERIALS FOR BOOTS.—For dress evening boots, patent leather; for dress morning boots, porpoise-hide; for ordinary walking, calf-skin; for gout, the best kid. Avoid grained and all enamelled leather.

CHAPTER VII.

HATS.

Hats—Best quality—White hats—Round hats—How to keep in good order.

THE hat of the day—or familiar chimney-pot—has been well abused and much written against. It is a favourite with no one, yet continues to hold its own against all comers. Why is this? Simply because those who inveigh against it are not prepared to suggest anything to take its place. With our present style of mufti it will be difficult to find a fitting substitute for it. A headdress for men, at once useful and ornamental, is not an easy thing to devise. Witness our army. Take the Line chako, the Rifle muff, the Fusilier busby, the Guards' bear-skin, the Cavalry helmet, and

the Lancer cap—throw in even the policeman's
wideawake—and say, from out the number, is
there one comfortable, graceful, useful, and not
ridiculous?

The difficulty of inventing a becoming headgear to tally with civilian dress is greater still.
Here follows a catalogue to choose from: The
Pork-pie hat; the Straw hat; the Wideawake;
the Sealskin; the Cloth cap, uniformly worn by
stokers and engine-drivers; the Rabbitskin, sacred
to the heads of costermongers; the Egyptian fez;
the Turkish turban; the Parsee cone; the Scotch
Glengarry; the Tyrolean hunter; the Spanish
sugarloaf; the Irish caubeen, &c. Now, fancy
yourself invited by H.R.H to a Chiswick garden
party, and had your pick out of the above list—
is there one you would select? I trow not. You
would be forced to fall back on that hideous
monstrosity, the black cowl of the period.

When the present style of hat came into fashion
I am not archæologist enough to say. The "Dic-
tionary of Universal Information" fixes the date
about 1795. Samuel Pepys, in his "Diary," dated
June 27th, 1660, states—"This day Mr. Holden
sent me a beaver, which cost me £4 5*s.* 0*d.*"
About the beginning of the eighteenth century,

the crowns of hats were mostly round, and had very broad brims, much resembling the Quaker hats, which rarely now are seen. In 1704 the regular three-cocked hat came into use, and held the sovereignty of head-coverings till about 1760, when a flat-topped hat, full brimmed, usurped its place. About thirty-five years after, the cylindrical hat now in general use came into vogue, and at the beginning of the nineteenth century was generally adopted, to the extinction of the cocked hat.

Your hat must not only be of best quality, but also in the fashion of the day. Why the phrase "as mad as a hatter," I know not, except it be that hatters are wayward, whimsical, and always fond of change — continually altering the style of headgear. A few leading hatters set the fashion in hats, and as the leading swells of the day patronize these exclusive few, and always wear good hats, we frequently see the style of hat changed. It evidently would not suit these first-class hatters to allow the same pattern to remain in fashion over-long. So one time the hat is bell-topped, with curly brim — anon cylindrical, and brim curtailed; hat-bands sometimes worn with buckle, other times in a

simple knot; brims and heights of this prepos-
terous cowl varying perhaps the one-sixteenth of
an inch from the fashion gone before. Things
were not much better in the reign of good Queen
Bess; for Stubbs writes thus of the hats of that
period :—"Sometimes they use them sharpe on
yᵉ crowne, peaking up like yᵉ speare of a steeple,
standing a quarter of a yarde above yᵉ crowne
of yᵉ head. Some others are flat and broade on
y crowne like yᵉ battlements of a house. Another
sorte have round crownes. Sometimes with one
kind of band, sometimes with another. Now
black, now white, now russet, now red, now green,
now yellow, now this, now that, never content
with one colour two days to an end." So, with
hatters' proverbial madness, there seems in all ages
to have been a uniformity of method in it. Be
this as it may, the laws of dress are inexorable,
and *you must wear the hat of the day, and purchase it from one of the few exclusive hatters.*

WHITE HATS are expensive wear. They suit
few so well as black. They cost nearly as much,
and cannot be "done up" more than once to
advantage. As to their being cooler than black
hats, this is fancy on the wearer's part, and shows
either faith enough to move mountains, or an

imagination more powerful than dynamite! To
wear a shabby black hat is a sign of poverty;
to wear a shabby white one indicates proceedings
in bankruptcy.

The round POT HAT is a grave difficulty. On
many occasions you must appear in it. Travelling
by rail or boat, the tall chimneypot is as much
out of place as a salmon on a gravel walk. Now,
I consider the present hard, inflexible round hat
(which will not pack like a gibus, but requires a
hat-case for itself) a most expensive article of
head-dress. You must have it of latest shape
(and how often they change fashion!) or you
will look like a grocer's errand boy, or "crooked-
legged conductor of a twopenny 'bus" out for a
holiday. A round hat of best quality costs about
sixteen shillings; it lasts a short time. After a
few showers of dust and rain its pristine beauty is
gone, and it will not bear doing up.

A hat when taken off should be hung up or
placed crown downwards on table or flat surface:
never, as the custom of some is, on its brim,
which operation tends to put it out of shape.
The leather of a hat should often be renewed.
A greasy leather, when seen, condemns a hat;
and besides, if greasy, the oil will ooze through

the silk, and necessitate the use of a mourning band to hush the matter up. Many people, free from family bereavements, suddenly "go into mourning for the King of Greece," as mild jokers feebly express it. The best coloured leather for wear is not of primrose tint, but more like Cayenne pepper. It should not be glazed; for on removing your hat you will look like the chief of an Indian tribe freshly oiled.

The treatment of a wet hat is a subject on which hat doctors differ. My mode of treatment, right or wrong, is as follows:

Wipe the humid tile with a clean silk handkerchief; and if only wet to windward, it must be equally damped to leeward and all round. Wipe away now until thoroughly dry and smooth. Before hanging it up, place it flat in hands, crown upwards, and pinch up equally with thumbs both sides of brim to restore its flaccid curl, then depress said brim slightly fore and aft. Hang it, if possible, in draughty passage until next day, for a hat thus treated takes a night to dry. Next morning attack it with very hard brush, and work away at it with a will. Should some slimy marks remain, as if a snail had left its track thereon, these can only be removed with a wire brush.

N.B.—Would you have your hat attain a ripe old age, avoid fingering the silk binding on the brim. See that the knot or buckle of band lies on the centre of the left side, and let the band itself be close "home" to the brim in its original position.

CHAPTER VIII.

SHIRTS.

White—Coloured—Flannel—Washing.

EAU BRUMMEL said, "A gentleman should show clean linen, and plenty of it." The first part of this sentence is strictly true, the second less so. There is no need, having a clean shirt on, to publish the fact, or to lead the public to infer you wear it as a disguise by undue exhibition of it. "Virtue is its own reward:" so the assumption of clean underclothing generally, even if its light be kept beneath a bushel, should afford the wearer the same pleasure as if ostentatiously paraded. When I see a man placarding his chest with a wide expanse of lawn, and exhibiting an unnecessary amount of cuffs, I infer he has got on neither a clean nor white shirt. The surmise generally proves correct. I often see in haberdashers' shops an exaggerated collar and lapel in one, designed to cover manly bosom. The commercial name of this impious fraud is called a Dickey. This felonious impostor must be made away with. No one with any self-respect can wear a dickey. A man clad in such an unmitigated imposition is a whited sepulchre of the very blankest type. If the reader knows any so depraved even to possess one, let him persuade the wretched man to pause, ere too late, in his headlong career—to burn the spurious rag, and he can then exclaim, with regenerated heart, "Richard" (not Dickey, mind) "is himself again!"

Many say, however, when this charge is brought against them, that they suffer from neuralgia, lumbago, and tic-douloureux, and the various other ailments that the afflicted Mrs. Elizabeth Waring was a martyr to, through having imprudently contracted the chronic habit of sleeping in a badly aired dormitory on the housetop. Well, what excuse is this? I do not prohibit flannel —wear an under flannel shirt—two if you like;

but you must cover it with an entire white shirt, not an aliquot part of it. If hypocrisy be the homage which vice pays to virtue, then the assumption of dickey is a sneaking admission of the necessity for showing clean linen, and a discreditable way of making a sham composition with the subject.

FLANNEL SHIRTS, to show, are only for country wear, or for those engaged in hard exercise, evolving that essential oil the outcome of Adam in pursuit of his daily bread and camombert.

OXFORD MATS will do for travelling ; and for all coloured shirts the collar should be of the same material as the shirt : white collar and cuffs over a coloured shirt is false heraldry, and excites suspicion that the extremities are clean and the garment itself dirty.

You should order two false collars for each coloured shirt.

Flannel shirts shrink every time washed. Before being made up the flannel should be wrung through hot water. Shirt-makers all will tell you *their* flannel will not shrink, or has already been shrunken. *Credat Judæus Apella*—don't you. In the selection of flannel, if you be a jolly bachelor and are not a judge of it, the maiden aunt before alluded to may help you. The collar-bands should be of grey holland, which will not shrink with the shirt, and on the arms, above elbows, should be two tucks (two inches), for letting down as the wristbands recede from view. At the time of making, a spare set of wristbands for each shirt should be cut, sewn, and put by, ready to replace the originals when too tight to button.

There is great art in shirt cutting; and no garment is much more uncomfortable and disquieting than a badly-cut shirt. The practice of buying ready-made shirts is not approved. Trusting merely to the neck measurement is fallacious, and by no means to be depended on. The breast and the shoulders of the shirt differ in dimensions, according to peculiarities in the figure, and both these must be attended to equally. Some persons blame their laundress for bad ironing, and accuse that functionary, often unjustly, for a wrinkled and puckered front, while the truth is they may be wearing a shirt so ill fitting as to defy all attempts to smooth it down. There is no economy in buying cheap shirts, nor, if there were, would it be right to encourage slop-shop dealers, who live and thrive by preying on the vitals of poor seamstresses.

A word on washing. Here let me condole with you, dear reader, on a severe domestic affliction, in which you have my heartfelt sympathy. We are hebdomadally at the mercy of a set of harpies, or furies, wise as serpents, compared with whom the witches in Macbeth are harmless as doves. I allude to the laundresses of the period, who mix up in their cauldron caustic ingredients that could only be appreciated by a Liebig or a Voëlckler. All haberdashers, assuredly, should subscribe freely to a fund, if it exists, for superannuated washerwomen, for they do the trade good service, and they know it. All the chlorides, alkalis, and mineral salts of modern science are employed by these regenerators of linen in their weekly cremation of our shirts. Fast colours they defy, stripes and coloured borders they simply laugh at. They fatten on sulphuric acid, and *potassa fusa* is to them but a mild stimulant. Would we could take the first Napoleon's advice, and wash our dirty linen at home—for our linen's sake.

I am free to confess I know no remedy against the ravages of these alchemists, except it be a

horsehair shirt, but am not monastic enough yet
to try it. On this subject the grand joke is—
better than all the burlesques of the day rolled
in one—that no living washerwoman ever admits
using these burning compounds! She has heard
of them—oh, yes! certainly. Many families—her
best customers—whose linen has been made a
holocaust—have left other laundresses and are
happy now with her. She lives in the country—
a pure purling brook runs by her door—soap
and starch (as used in the Royal laundry—and
she takes care she gets it) are the only articles
used by this simple-minded party. *Splendide
mendax!* Could you search her *sanctum*, you
would find, beside the bottle of gin necessary for
cleaning irons, enough chemicals to start a dry-
salter in business, and corrosive sublimates suffi-
cient to cauterize creation!

CHAPTER IX.

MISCELLANEOUS.

Gloves—Ties—'Kerchiefs—Collars—Gaiters—Jewellery—
Umbrellas.

GLOVES.

HOW much can be spent on the trivialities of dress, and how small a return the outlay yields! Thank goodness! the day is gone by—I hope for ever—when a man's position was compromised if seen with ungloved hands. Twenty years ago, had one ventured into that resort of *gandins* and *cocottes*—the Burlington Arcade—your best friend would have felt bound in the interests of fashion to cut you dead, had you not shown *ganté* with Jouvin's best kids.

At present there is rather a revulsion in favour of the naked fist; and although gloves in winter are almost a necessity for comfort, one can please oneself to wear them or not.

It is a ridiculous custom to carry gloves in the hand—merely to convince the passers-by you have a pair; there is no practical object attained by so doing. Either wear them *on* the hand, or stow them altogether. At *matinées*, garden parties, and resorts where ladies go, gloves are necessary; but a man can go a whole season through Clubland ungloved—not even seised of a pair—without losing caste in modern society. I own tight-fitting gloves look very elegant and *chic;* but it will be found on analysis they afford more satisfaction to their wearer than to the outside world.

If you wear lavender kids, or those of *coleur tendre*, they must be of the best quality. If *foncé*, and double-stitched, they need not be so expensive. I recommend to the reader's notice the Danish gloves, now extensively imported. As a rule they are excellent for wear, and about half the cost of French gloves.

As to having gloves cleaned, I consider the game not worth the candle. I have tried it, but unsuccessfully. After half an hour's struggle to get in, *plus* five minutes' wear, the finger-tips invariably suggested the idea of my having dipped them into a pot of raspberry preserve.

To have gloves dyed any colour than black is a waste of money ; then they should be two sizes too large for you, as they are safe to shrink in the process.

TIES.

In these you will find an infinite variety— quite an *embarrass* of choice. No tie or scarf can be neater than plain black in silk or satin. If you are well dressed, it looks perfection ; if indifferently, it attracts no notice. In summer a chaste effect is produced by wearing a French crape handkerchief or *foulard* passed through an ebony ring. If you insist on a fancy tie, I suggest a black ground with lavender or mauve sprig or stripe.

It was a glorious epoch in the annals of dress when the present fashion of scarf, a made-up sailor's knot, came into vogue. All the trouble of folding, knotting, and tying is done away, and the use of breastpin dispensed with. Long may the present fashion flourish! For neatness, dispatch, and comfort, it **cannot** be improved on.

Here let me lift up my voice and cry aloud against the custom which obtains, at the University boat race time, for every howling cad to fly the colours of either University. For those connected with either seat of learning, or for the friends of the rival crews, of course, it is proper "form" to sport their distinguishing colours; but for others in no way concerned with either to follow suit is a proceeding idiotic, snobbish, and as much devoid of reason as it would be for any man, not in the service, to commemorate the birthday of H.R.H. the Duke of Cambridge by walking in Rotten Row clad in evening dress and a military shako.

———

POCKET HANDKERCHIEFS.

On these useful nasal attendants I have known men expend fancy sums—seven shillings and sixpence each, and four shillings for crest embroidered thereon. You cannot dress with

economy if you indulge in luxuries at this rate.
I can buy good cambric kerchiefs for from twelve
to eighteen shillings a dozen; excellent for wear,
and quite good enough to lose, or—same thing
—to lend to a catarrhic friend.

Laundresses are not over-particular in return-
ing good handkerchiefs; and should you find a
strange one when the weekly tale of washing
comes back, the odds are against its being of
superior quality to the one for which it has been
substituted. This remark may be made general,
and applied to all articles confided to her care.

The *blanchisseuse* of the day is unlearned in
Homeric lore, and seldom follows the example
of him who once gave gold for brass.

Memo.— Shun handkerchiefs with illustrated
devices, portraying *pseudo* likenesses of the recent
Derby winner, the Hon. Member for Stoke-upon-
Orton, the last fashionable murderer, or latest
celebrity added to Madame Tussaud's Chamber
of Horrors.

COLLARS.

Always get the best quality, and entrust their
regeneration to a laundress of probity and

intelligence. Show at least an inch of white border over and above your coat-collar. After my remark on white vests *(quod vide)* is it necessary to caution you against paper collars? They are the abomination of desolation spoken of by all the prophets.

I repeat here what I have elsewhere said, that with coloured shirts collars should be worn of the same material, and that it is advisable, when ordering fancy shirts, to have duplicate sets to each. Often in the heat of summer the collar becomes limp and flaccid, while the shirt remains spotless and without blemish. Hence the reason. Why change the shirt for sake of one collar?

GAITERS

Are very much in vogue since the fashion to wear them was set in high quarters. If you suffer from cold feet, and feel a necessity for extra pedal covering, there is no objection to them; but to wear them simply because H.R.H. does so is silly and snobbish in the extreme. To fancy that a badly-cut gaiter over a worse cut boot can bestow any *éclat* on any one is a

delusion allied to mental aberration, and the idea
that drab spatterdashes, purchased ready made
in the Tottenham Court Road, will make people
believe you belong to the staff of Marlborough
House is an hallucination to deceive oneself only.
You might as well have a lesson or so on the
violin, and hope to pass off for the Duke of
Edinburgh.

I once knew a man (weak minded) who fancied
himself a walking edition of the *Court Circular*,
and gave his opinion on matters of *haut ton* as a
Deus ex machinâ.   He based his pretentions for
so doing on the slender fact of his employing
the ramoneur to the Royal Family to sweep his
chimneys.   But was he more ridiculous than
those who wear gaiters solely in imitation of an
illustrious Prince?

———

JEWELLERY.

If you wear jewellery, let it be limited in
quantity, and of the best quality.   Beyond a
gold chain for watch, I do not see the necessity
for any.   In these days of aluminium and oroide,
gold studs and links cease to be ornamental, and

are better replaced by mother-o'-pearl, *onyx*, or other real stone. A profusion of jewellery, real or mock, will cause you to be handicapped as a Jew bill discounter, or that hybrid non-descript,—bankrupt cigar merchant and general financial agent.

I should always mistrust the man who in cold blood goes in for mock jewellery. Nothing short of half rations or impending starvation would induce me to stretch my legs beneath his maho-gany. Beware of him when he plays the part of Amphytrion. He cannot well adulterate the solids, but in the matter of fluids look out! for here his imitative talent will assert itself ruth-lessly, to the cost of the interior economy of your vitals. The pale sherry he offers you will be a triumph of modern chemistry, and derive its origin, not from Andalusia, but from the more accessible region of Bethnal Green. Beware of his champagne! he is fooling thee. Think you the parent of this excitable potion ever flour-ished in the land where the Franco-Prussian war has lately raged? Would it unman an annexed Alsatian, aggrieved at German rule, by remind-ing him of his mother country? I trow not. It probably has its birthplace in Rotherhithe, and

the market gardens around that classic spot
supply the rhubarb, which, let us hope, is the most
harmless ingredient in its composition. Touch
not his *vieux Cognac*. It very likely is methy-
lated spirit, dashed with a flavouring of fusil oil
—known to the Jews in the east of London
under the euphonious title of Whitechapel Finish.

There are different degrees of heinousness in
the assumption of mock jewellery; and the more
valuable be the article imitated, the greater is
the moral guilt of the wearer. To wear an
illegitimate Albert chain for real is equivalent,
when reduced to figures—its simplest terms
—to leading the public to infer that you carry
as portable property ten pounds' worth of
bullion, while the cost of the spurious cable
could not have exceeded 10s. To wear mock
brilliants—say, imitation diamonds—either in
rings or studs, implies the issue of a false pro-
spectus on your part, tacitly stating you have a
paid-up capital of £100 about your person, while
the fictitious gems, whatever they may have cost,
are not value for one hundred pence. Nor, if
detected in the latter nefarious transaction, can
you urge a valid excuse, nor advance anything
in arrest of judgment or in mitigation of your

crime. The impostor with the duffing chain might say he had it for the protection of his watch against pickpockets and the light-fingered fraternity. This would be a weak set-off. A steel chain will answer this purpose, and always looks well, for it is what it professes to be, and nothing more. But the deliberate assumption of paste or false stones in rings, studs, solitaires, or breastpins, " the same with intent to deceive," cannot be palliated, and leaves the wearer convicted of a delinquency not markedly dissimilar to the smasher's art.

Wearing mock jewellery is not a commercial forgery, but still a moral fraud. It is uttering spurious metal, and, being deceitful above all things, must be desperately wicked.

UMBRELLAS.

" The English have weather, but no climate," said M. Talleyrand some years ago, and to the present day the necessity exists to be always armed with an umbrella in this country.

The French say, "*Les Anglais quittent quelque fois leurs femmes, mais leurs parapluies, jamais !*"

and however true this remark may be, it unfortunately happens that a judicial separation or divorce often takes place between the Englishman and his favourite.

It is easier to keep one's temper than one's umbrella. I have often wondered, in these days of limited companies, it has never occurred to some brilliant promoter to launch "The Mutual Co-operative Umbrella Guarantee Company" to insure the public in the quiet and peaceable possession of this useful implement. At clubs an excellent plan prevails of placing one glove on top of umbrella handle in the rack, retaining the other in your possession on the principle of the counterfoil in a bank cheque. A man must be mentally and morally abstracted to appropriate under these circumstances both glove and umbrella as his own; and if you detect one in the act, you will be justified in saying to him, as Wellington did to Huskisson, "It is no mistake, it can be no mistake, and it shall be no mistake."

The best stuff for wear is Italian twilled silk; and I advise my readers to have two umbrellas, one for real work on confirmed wet days, the other for dress occasions; and both should be kept thoroughly clean, and all mud-spots removed therefrom by the use of sponge.

CHAPTER X.

THE TOILET.

Tubbing — Shampooing — Hair Revivers — Scent — Soap — Receipts.

FEEL no moral obligation whatever to write a chapter on the toilet, yet I do it in that excess of philanthropy with which I am surcharged. In fact, I am beginning to take an interest in you, as an artist warms to his work and becomes enamoured of his subject; and as to dress as a gentleman requires neatness in person as well as in clothes, I throw in some hints on the toilet without extra charge. Of course, if you think you are having more than your shilling's worth, and feel uneasy at the fact, it is competent for you to do as many proper-minded people act towards the Chancellor of the

Exchequer, and send conscience-money to me, addressed care of my worthy publishers. The proceeds, if any, will be devoted to a most excellent charity, and dispensed on the principle of that axiom which says "Charity begins at home."

I am now going to put a startling question to you—for I take nothing for granted—"Reader, do you tub?" If not, I had liefer you would throw this book away than make me accessory to the fact of your trying to dress as a gentleman in an unregenerated state. Repent you of your sins in sackcloth and ashes rather than continue to cover up pollution with outward show of purple and fine linen. The old adage declares that "Cleanliness is next to Godliness;" and although you may not find it an easy matter to go through the eye of a needle, in all conscience soap and water should be within your grasp. Some men, at heart hydrophobists, acquire by false pretences a character for cleanliness they little merit. I know some who have their daily bath (filled, at all events), not that they like it, but because they fear it will be bruited that they do not wash, and, with a quart of water in their tub, manage to flounder about, and make more splash than Captain Webb in all his trip across the Channel.

Do you anoint yourself with oil, and use those filthy stearine compounds known in the adipose trade as pomatum? If so, *cui bono?* Do you wish to emulate a butcher's apprentice in his unctuous hankering after grease? Do you believe in their power to reproduce hair on bald pates? If so, and to shake your faith in capillary attraction, to disabuse your mind that grey hairs can be changed except by dye or death, I will a plain unvarnished tale unfold:

My friend, Major Bangalore, came back to England, having been quartered for a long time (three lustres quite) in India. If it be true (which no doubt it is) that all the hairs of our head are numbered, poor Bangalore's bill for celestial stationery would be nothing, as it would not have required one line in folio for the recording angel to enter in the grand total of bristles on his cranium-top. In fact, he looked, with hat off, as if he had made the insane attempt to bolt the plain ball at billiards, and failing to swallow it, it was working its way out of the summit of his knowledge-box. One day he visited a temple devoted to the hair-cutting art—not one hundred miles from the Burlington Arcade — to get his residuary fringe trimmed, and placed himself beneath the deft shears of the cunning operator. The usual stereotyped dialogue took place (so old, we wonder any are entrapped by it; yet, remember, every week we read in the press of the "confidence dodge," and find flats abound daily to be practised on). His hair was thin on the top; yes, he knew it—hopelessly gone. Oh, no! none need despair, if they would only use the miraculous Balm of Gilead; hair must be induced, even on the palm of the hand, if regularly applied, &c., &c.

Bangalore, all this while, humoured the artist, who, thinking he had landed a good thing, produced testimonials from Lord B— and Viscount C—, testifying that they had been bald as coots, but through using the Gilead Mixture they now were hairy like Absalom—only rather more so—and requesting the perfumer to send without delay some depilatory as an antidote against their redundant frizziness. The Major inquired what articles he would require; so the *coiffeur* looked him out a pair of electric brushes, porcelain saucers, Turkey sponges mounted in ivory, knicknacks various; to apply a pot of Gilead's Balm, and a carboy of fluid, called wash, with an unpronounceable bastard classic name that would have tripped up any Oxford don, and made a member of the London School Board resign his seat for shame. The price of all told was five pounds odd. Said Bangalore, "Do you guarantee the use of these will completely restore my hair?" Certainly he did. He would swear it, or make affidavit to that effect, if the Major preferred that form of security better. Him answering, the swift-footed Bangalore addressed (for, cunning veteran! he planned a speedy retreat), and spoke in winged words:

"Here is my card—Smith & Junior, erst of Cornhill, are my agents—I refer you to them. I shall not pay you now, but am ready to sign a stamped agreement, to pay you, not five pound odd, but twenty-five pounds, if your specifics restore my hair within twelve months."

"No, thank you, sir," replied the assistant, quietly putting back the goods; "we don't do business on those terms."

Bangalore lost his chance that time, and to this day remains as bald as ever!

Much money is frittered away on scents, essences, and fatty matters in perfumers' shops; and however excusable in the fair sex to waste their substance on such trash, it is a positive sin for the sterner sex to dissipate their coin in cosmetics and perfumed investments. Until the Millennium come there can be no excuse advanced for men purchasing even a box of spikenard. Is there an object more supremely beneath contempt than a male—no matter what his age—making himself up with rouge, hare's foot, and violet powder—pencilling his eyebrows, waxing his moustache, brilliantining his beard, and trying to be, *à la* Rachel, beautiful for ever? How ridiculous, too, is the process of shampooing at a hairdresser's! I do not disapprove of washing the hair, but object to confining the times of doing it to the periodical visits made for hair-cutting. The hair should be shampooed every day in the domestic bath. You might as well limit the periods of toe-nail cutting to the seasons for ordering new boots, and expect your boot-maker to do the paring for you; or only wash your face when you sit for your *carte de visite*, and make the photographer perform the ceremony himself.

No, be not deceived; the best cosmetic for gentlemen is soap; and the best soap is plain unscented yellow, or elder-flower if you prefer it.

As to other toilet requisites, tooth powder and

hairwash may be allowed. I append receipts for these, and premise that from two to three shillings annually will suffice for both.

Soft soap is an excellent detergent, and, dissolved in warm water, should be used for shampooing—well sponging off afterwards in cold water.

Take—

Rectified Spirits of Wine	. Seven ounces.
Liquid Ammonia .	. Three ,,
Glycerine . . .	. One ,,

Mix, and let a lotion be made. Apply it to the roots of the hair with a small sponge. If too strong, dilute it with water.

Take—

Powdered Myrrh .	. Two ounces.
Bicarbonate of Potass	. Two ,,
Powdered Cuttlefish .	. Two ,,

Mix, and apply with an ordinary tooth-brush. This need not be used more than on alternate days.

CHAPTER XI.

OLD CLOTHES.

T is very easy to be liberal at the expense
of other people, so if you ask me what
to do with your old clothes, I should
say, give away what you don't want in charity.
You may act on this advice or not—that is your
affair, not mine. Some sell their clothes, when
antiquated or past their own wearing, to itinerant
dealers from the other side of Jordan. As a rule
they give little or nothing for them. The deal,
if any, "not enricheth you," but certainly does
not "make them poor indeed." If you know any
deserving, broken-down, struggling, poor devil of
a fellow who has seen better days—they are
easily found!—let him have your cast-off ward-

robe; and what may be seedy in your own eyes will warm his heart and soul, and turn him out, instead of a patchwork of darns and tatters, in a comparative style of Oriental splendour. An old overcoat, like charity, will often cover a multitude of sins and defects in underclothing. There are several charitable institutions which invite the benevolent to send them any sort of cast-off garments for distribution in inclement weather. The ladies and gentlemen who superintend these excellent depôts have on their lists the names of needy and really deserving persons, so I hope you will be generous with your *exuviæ*, and let some one have the benefit of your moulting.

There is more real charity in dispensing warm clothing, blankets, and bubbling hot soup in cold weather to those who need it (God knows, their name is legion!) than in heading subscription lists for polyglots for the Squashibaws, and moral tracts for those who can't read to make pipe-lights of.

After this homily, which will no doubt receive a proper amount of theoretical consideration, we come to the practical view of old clothes; and **as the devil** is said not to be so black as he is painted, so I affirm old clothes are not generally so shabby as supposed.

I will give you a wrinkle before you discard old clothes as past all hope of wear. Look up the best of them, and put them on one side. Separate the sheep from the goats, and if they be not torn or worn white at seams, they may yet do you good service at trifling cost and little trouble. The *modus operandi* is:—Enlist into your service for a short period—on the present military system—a lad of broad shoulders and well-developed biceps. You need not go beyond the shoeblack brigade in search of a recruit. Provide him with the following tools:—A cane or limber switch, a hard brush, and a clean kitchen table. Let him thoroughly dust and brush your clothes once, then, to make sure certain, make him repeat the process until you are satisfied no grit remains behind. This must be done "with a will," and the switch well laid on, even as prison warders flog garotters, not as if whisking flies off the back of Venus. You may now supply him with the following chemicals and the means of using them:—Liquid ammonia, spirits of turpentine, and benzoline. With a piece of cloth list or flannel dipped in ammonia, every speck or spot of grease must first be carefully removed by dint of hard rubbing. Then a pad is made of clean flannel—same colour as the cloth to be operated upon — filled with cloth shreds or cotton wool to the size of an ordinary white turnip. Take equal parts of benzoline and turps in a soup-plate, and with the pad half-saturated, rub from collar down one way all the garment over.

This work is no child's play. The mixture must be freely used; every part of the cloth must be hard rubbed, and elbow-grease must not be spared. When your clothes are thoroughly done, they must be hung up in a draught or open air, and a week will elapse before they lose their smell. Then look them over, and any worth keeping must be sent to your jobbing tailor for buttons, repairs, &c.; and last, not least, a through damping, and hotpressing with the iron.

I am dead against sending soiled coats, &c., to scourers. I have often seen it tried, but never with success. I grant they send them back beautiful to behold, but they are not worth the cost. Scourers have a knack of rubbing up the pile and getting a peach-like bloom upon it. This is fleeting and transitory, and after one shower of rain or dust the garment is done for beyond redemption.

N.B.—Always have liquid ammonia in your possession, to remove stains on your coat-front caused by the trickling from moustache or beard.

Before putting away your clothes after summer or winter for the next six months, have them well dusted and sponged with benzoline. This will effectually stay the ravages of moth. I have tried pepper, salt, mustard, and all the round of the cruet, without success; and I verily believe that Worcester sauce and pickles added would be powerless against their fret.

CHAPTER XII.

CONCLUSION.

 WORD in season to wind up with.
There is a time for all things, and much
depends on selecting suitable seasons
for ordering new costume. There must be a
method in your moulting—properly defined
periods for sloughing your coat skin. Some
of feeble intelligence will burst out with a brand
new winter overcoat in the month of April—
only, say, to shelve it the following month until
next winter, having perhaps passed the previous
quarter in a state of semi-seediness; or, after
getting through the height of the season with last
year's toggery, will break out the end of July

with a fig-out which would have dazzled Rotten Row if ordered earlier on.

There are certain times of year when good clothes should be brought out sparingly. Beware the Ides of March. Its driving winds blowing grit and triturated stones, followed up with hail and storms of rain, will take the bloom off everything, a Mackintosh excepted. March and April are excellent months in which to hack the least prized specimens of your wardrobe. During this period the process of incubation may go safely on, and culminate in a general bursting of the shell and grand transformation scene, the month of May.

What saith Spenser ?—

> " Then came fair May, the fairest mayde on earth,
>   Deckt all with dainties of her season's pride,
>   And throwing flowers out of her lap around."

I advise you to follow the "fairest mayde's" example, and turn from chrysalis into butterfly this month. Old clothes done up will not pass muster, May. The bright glint of day will search out all imperfections, and discover the weak spots in your rehabilitation.

Now look up your best morning coat, and let

the trousers of sombre hue give way to those of light and airy tint. The eventful moment has arrived for the heavy-shod laced-up Balmoral to abdicate in favour of the highly lacquered light-soled boot. Patent leather shoes may now be worn, lined with striped or fancy socks; but if the pedal proportions of the wearer be on elephantine scale—beef to the heel—this form of *chaussure* should not be chosen.

About the Derby time, I notice, most young men flare up elaborately to attend that cockney carnival of costermongers. Let me warn my readers against exposing their elegance at Epsom. I can understand proper-minded persons dressing to the nines for aristocratic Ascot or glorious Goodwood ; but there is no more occasion to turn out "swell" for Epsom, than to sit down in full evening dress at an eighteenpenny ordinary with bagmen.

Before our subject is concluded, you may ask —Is it necessary to be so particular about one's dress? I answer, YES. Thank goodness! the days of foppery are passed, and the terms "dandy," "exquisite," and "buck" are banished to the limbo of oblivion. Time in this practical age is too valuable to waste over the knot of a cravat; and a "basketful of failures" would now be thought a poor day's work. Still, there is a style and standard of dress which obtains among gentlemen, and if you move in their sphere, it is all the better to conform to it.

In point of fact, if you hold a certain position you are bound to dress after the fashion of the day, not only for your own self-respect, but as a homage to society. Of course, if you are exalted above the vulgar herd, you can afford to dress as you like, but I do not think you will enhance your position by affecting any eccentricity in attire. I often see, as I take my walks abroad on "the shady side of Pall Mall," ex-Cabinet Ministers and Teutonic Generals Serenely High, wrapped in swaddling-clothes (I cannot call them dressed), in such condition that were a Semitic merchant who deals in old clo' to give half a sovereign for their amalgamated kits, he would lose money by the transaction. On the other hand, I could point out some of the most brilliant men living who were leaders of fashion in their day, and who are still remarkable, on the Bench, in the House, or in Camp, for the neatness and precision of their dress.

I know that poets, painters, and professors

often affect a careless *abandon*, perhaps to attract attention ; and so long as this *negligé* is confined to badly-cut clothes, let them follow the dictates of their fancies; but if it assumes the proportions of habitual neglect of ablutions and sanitary precautions, it is time to protest against the practice.

It may be my opacity, but I fail to see any antagonism between high mental culture and well-polished boots, or why the term *savant* should be dissociated from *savon*, or from soap and water.

INDEX.

T. W. DORÉ,

Court Tailor,

25 CONDUIT ST., AND 36 GEORGE ST.,
HANOVER SQUARE,

Uses none but the Best Materials, and keeps a Large Assortment of the Latest Novelties always in Stock. Every attention is paid to the wishes of the Customer, and *all Garments are cut and made by experienced Workmen*, careful regard being given to the prevailing Style, and the taste and requirements of the wearer.

Price List.

	£	s.	d.
Improved Ulster	3	3	0
Frock Coat	4	10	0
Vest	1	0	0
Trousers	1	8	0
Dress Coat	4	4	0
Do. Vest	1	1	0
Do. Trousers	1	15	0
Morning Coat	3	10	0
Do. Vest	0	15	0
Winter Overcoat	4	10	0
Summer do.	2	10	0
Suit of Dittos	4	4	0

The Livery Department continues to receive special attention, and Gentlemen who are particular as to the fit and style of their Servants' Clothes are respectfully solicited to favour it with a trial.

Terms: Five per Cent. Discount for Cash on delivery.

25 CONDUIT ST., AND 36 GEORGE ST.,
HANOVER SQUARE.

THE CHANDOS LIBRARY.

A SERIES OF STANDARD WORKS IN ALL CLASSES OF LITERATURE.

In crown 8vo, price 3*s*. 6*d*. each, cloth gilt.

The Percy Anecdotes. By REUBEN and SHOLTO PERCY.
Verbatim Reprint of Original Edition. Introduction by JOHN TIMBS.
Original Steel Portraits, and Index. Three Vols., each Complete in itself.

Book of the Church. By ROBERT SOUTHEY, LL.D. With
Notes from the "Vindiciæ Ecclesiæ Anglicanæ."

Pepys' Diary and Correspondence. With Seven Steel Portraits
arranged as a Frontispiece, Memoir, Introductory Preface, and full Index.

Abbeys, Castles, and Ancient Halls of England and Wales.
Their Legendary Lore and Popular History—South, Midland, North. By
JOHN TIMBS, Author of "Curiosities of London," and ALEXANDER GUNN.
New Frontispiece. Three Vols. Each Volume Complete in itself.

Johnson's Lives of the Poets; with Critical Observations on
their Works, and a Sketch of the Author's Life by Sir WALTER SCOTT.
Steel Frontispiece.

Book of Authors : A Collection of Criticisms, Ana, Mots, Personal Descriptions, &c. By W. CLARK RUSSELL.

Evelyn's Diary and Correspondence. Edited by BRAY. 784 pp.
With Frontispiece and full Index.

Gibbon.—The Life and Correspondence of Edward Gibbon.
With his History of the Crusades. Verbatim Reprint, and copious Index.
Steel Portrait.

Representative Actors : A Collection of Criticisms, Anecdotes,
Personal Descriptions, &c. &c.

Gibbon's Decline and Fall of the Roman Empire. With
Portrait. Three Vols.

Life of William Hutton, of Birmingham, and the Hutton Family.
Compiled and Edited by LLEWELLYNN JEWITT, F.S.A. Steel Portrait.

A Century of Anecdote. Compiled and Edited by JOHN TIMBS.
With Frontispiece.

The Romance of London. By JOHN TIMBS. Two Vols. With
Frontispiece.

Merry England in the Olden Time. By GEORGE DANIEL.
With Illustrations by JOHN LEECH and ROBERT CRUIKSHANK.

Bartholomew Fair: Its Complete History, &c. By HENRY
MORLEY. With Original Illustrations.

Scott's (Sir Walter) Lives of Eminent Novelists and Drama-
tists. With Additional Notes and Portrait.

Scott's (Sir Walter) Essays on Chivalry, Romance, and the
Drama. With Portrait.

Pope's Homer's Iliad and Odyssey. FLAXMAN's Illustrations.

The Spanish Ballads. Translated by J. B. LOCKHART, LL.B.
And The Chronicle of the Cid, by ROBERT SOUTHEY. With Portraits.

Don Quixote, Life and Adventures of. By CERVANTES.
With Illustrations.